- JPhillips -

What Are People Saying About SOAR®?

"Your program helped me change into an A student after struggling with C's and D's. I'm looking forward to using it in college!"
- Chelsea S., 12th grade student

"WHY DIDN'T SOMEONE TELL ME ABOUT THIS BEFORE?"
- Stephen G., 11th grade student

"The feedback received from this book has been awesome! They absolutely loved it."
-Elissa L., 6th grade counselor

"Good examples, well-organized and researched, including 'helpful hints' like locker organization, how to talk to teachers, etc."
- Scott B, high school teacher

"Once I learned how to get control over what I was supposed to learn before a test and what to do on a test I was so much more confident!"
- Sachi I., 11th grade student

"This is more useful and interesting than any other class!"
- Shane D., 9th grade student

"Homework is getting done faster and there is much less fighting in our household!"
- Michael Z., 9th grade student

"The SOAR® system is working! There have been no missed assignments and no problems with homework being left behind."
- Vicki W., teacher

"I feel much more in control when I study now because I know exactly what to do. I don't waste time staring at my textbook, I take better notes in class, and I am better prepared for each class so when I study for a test, it all comes together."
- Katlyn R., 11th grade student

"SOAR® has been very successful. It is a very purposeful, well-constructed program, and it has great potential to develop student responsibility, develop student thinking, and develop their autonomy in owning their own schoolwork and taking pride in it."
- Tobi F., middle school principal

D1411182

Who Is Using SOAR®?

SOAR® Study Skills is the best-selling study skills book in the world!

The *SOAR® Curriculum* is in 3,600 + schools across the USA

and 30 nations worldwide! To see a more detailed list, visit: www.studyskills.com/map

Teachers Declare SOAR® 98.9% Effective !in Improving Student Performance

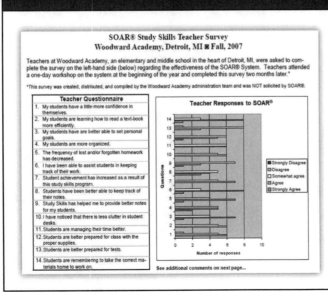

Teachers were asked to complete a survey regarding the effectiveness of the SOAR® system.

This survey was created, distributed, and compiled by a school administration team and was NOT solicited by SOAR®.

For more details, visit:
www.studyskills.com/effective

SOAR® Learning & Soft Skills:
Proven to Raise GPAs by an Average of One Full Point!

Maeser Prep Academy introduced SOAR® to their 6th graders and was eager to share their results with us. (We did not solicit this data from them in any way.) They purchased the program then contacted us with their stellar results at the end of the school year!

Their report...

- **"GPAs were up at least a full point!"**

- **"Test scores are five points above the national average** and five standard points beyond students' previous scores, which is TREMENDOUS growth in these students...."

Maeser Prep Principal, Robyn Ellis, explained why she invests in SOAR®:

This is a win-win! SOAR® encompasses the entire curriculum. *It doesn't just teach "one more thing." It teaches students HOW to learn. So, once [students] learn how to learn, they can engage in all of the subject areas. It encompasses everything; they don't just use it in one class, they use it in every class.*

And they are going to use it every day of every month of every year throughout their entire educational experience. *Then, they are going to use [these skills] in their careers and to better their communities. So, to not do this program because, "Oh, maybe it's expensive to buy the books." It is <u>not an option</u> anymore for us. We realize what a valuable piece of the curriculum this is, and it would be detrimental not to do this.*

If you are considering this program, I would say, whole-heartedly, this is a definite "YES!" *This is something that will compliment any curriculum, any program, any school because it gives students <u>life</u> skills. This is something they are going to use throughout their life. I would whole-heartedly encourage anyone to embrace this and add this to their curriculum!*

Congratulations to the team of educators at Maeser Prep Academy for creating successful outcomes for their students now...and investing in their future!

Teachers:

Have you accessed your Multi-Media Teacher's Guide?

This book is provided with a license to use our Multi-Media Teacher's Guide including:

- 240+ Slides
- Four types of assesments
- Multi-Media extension activities
- Embedded videos
- Links to additional online content

Access to the Multi-Media Teacher's Guide is emailed to you at the time of purchase. If you have not recieved that email (check your "junk" folder), contact us at info@studyskills.com with:

- Your name
- School name/Distrcit name

We will confirm your license and respond with your access to the MMTG within 2-3 days.

FREE Book Bonus Materials!
Visit: www.StudySkills.com/bonus-edu

See references throughout this book for additional, multi-media resources available at the web page above.

SOAR

LEARNING & SOFT SKILLS
FOR COLLEGE & CAREER READINESS

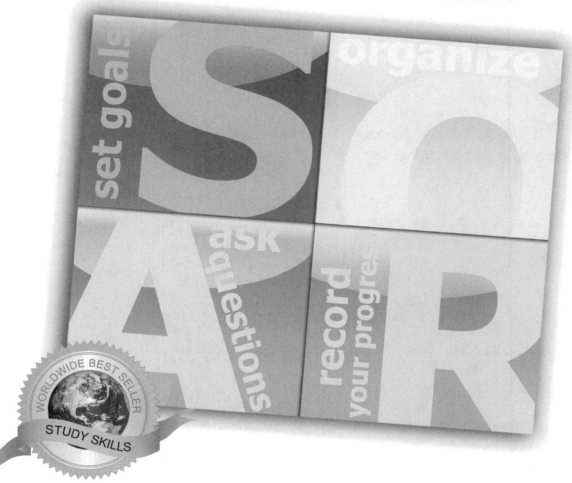

set goals

organize

ask questions

record your progress

WORLDWIDE BEST SELLER
STUDY SKILLS

"Better grades in less time!"

SUSAN KRUGER, M.Ed.

Designed by Susan Kruger
Illustrations by Karl Mayry
Photographs by Dan Kruger, Cathy Scott Stoey, Brian Woodcock
Graphic Illustrations by Susan Kruger

Internet: www.StudySkills.com
Email: info@StudySkills.com

Published by Grand Lighthouse Publishing, Lake Orion, MI

Library of Congress Control Number: 2005935199
ISBN - 10: 0-9774280-5-2
ISBN - 13: 978-0-9774280-5-2
SAN: 257-6570

Printed in the United States of America

To the best parents a kid could ask for:

Mom—*who weathered countless homework storms before
I learned all of this information.*

Dad—*who always encouraged me to "stick to my guns."*

And to the best husband a girl could ask for:

Brian—*a great teacher in the classroom...and in life.*

Dedication

Table of Contents

This book has been evolving since the day I started first grade and cried every night about my homework. (Sorry, Mom!) The greatest asset I have in writing this book is that I have been a student for a *very* long time and struggled in school for many years.

Thank you to **Pam Romanelli, Sr. Elena Sabulusky,** and **Sr. Cecilia Bondy,** who opened their doors at Divine Child for the very first SOAR® workshop! I am so grateful for your faith in me!

To all of the students who have attended the SOAR® workshops and classes over the years…I am grateful for your active participation, open minds, fabulous suggestions, and gracious feedback. Your energy and enthusiasm help me constantly improve and move SOAR® to new heights.

Donna Bednarczyk…in a simple act of kindness, you gave my career wings. You are a constant source of encouragement and great "mommy mentor." To Luke…it was an honor to be your teacher. Your mom says that my "Marky stories" are very similar to her "Luke stories." If that means that Mark grows up to be such a nice young man, I am a very lucky mom.

Ginelle Barry…Thank you for graciously bringing peace to our household, trouble-shooting software, and editing photos and illustrations. You are an amazing role model; I am proud to be your friend.

Cathy Scott Stoey…I am grateful for your genuine support and encouragement. You were exceptionally generous with your time and talents in the last few months of the project, taking/editing photos, and reassuring me that it would all turn out okay. Thank you!

Karl Mayry…Your incredible talent has helped this book come to life! Thank you for all of your drawings and for being so gracious with re-drawings. You are one of my strongest sources of encouragement; thank you for being a true friend to our family and a fabulous mentor to Mark.

I am lucky to have two amazing brothers and a sister-in-law to call upon for a variety of help. Dan, Greg, and Amanda…thank you for all of your help with computer problems, websites, photo-taking, photo-editing, and reviewing/editing this book. I am so grateful that you are all so gracious about giving help; your support means the world to me!

Grandpa Willer…your stories of entrepreneurship and words of encouragement were invaluable. You always had faith in my work!

Mom and Dad Woodcock…This project would have taken another five years to complete without your help. Your gracious, endless help allowed me to write this book. Mom, thank you for reviewing the book and yes, your delicious homemade chocolate chip cookies kept me happy and energized.

Acknowledgments

Mom and Dad Kruger...this book is dedicated to both of you in recognition for the great foundation you provided throughout my life. However, I must also thank you for all of your help in getting this book off the ground! All of the babysitting, meals, household projects, and editing were invaluable contributions. Mom, thank you for offering to do "whatever it took" to help me make my deadline. Dad, thanks for your valuable input on the cover design.

Mark...you have a beautiful spirit and are a brave warrior. You have transformed my mission and vision for SOAR®! I am honored to be your mom!

Madison...I've wanted a baby girl since the day Uncle Greg was born! (I was 4-1/2 and wanted to send him back to the hospital because he was a boy. Of course, I've since decided that Uncle Greg is pretty cool!) You are such a blessing in my life. You arrived a few years after the first edition of this book was published, but SOAR® exploded the day you were born. You certainly have been my "God-luck" charm! I love you.

My SOAR® team...several people have contributed to my team since the first edition of this book was published. I want to especially thank Kevin Stone and Jessie Smude for all of their work and dedication to providing excellent service to each other and our clients.

Finally, to Brian...You have been instrumental in every aspect of SOAR® from the beginning. You were good for the ideas when the program was first created and have never failed to bail me out of creative slumps since. I could never thank you enough for all of the sacrifices you have made. You are an amazing father and make being a mom very enjoyable. You keep this trip fun...I love you!

Dear Fellow Educator,

Why Do You Have to Work *So* Hard to Make Students Learn?

You work harder and harder, but clearly feel a drag. You are tasked with more things to do, document, and correlate every day. Your extended efforts never seem to be enough. Students become more apathetic.

Many people are quick to blame technology, but that's not it. There is something much more significant going on.

The "New Initiative" Bandwagon

In an effort to "fix" the problem, politicians and school systems usher in new "initiatives" to improve instruction and *finally* make things better. These initiatives are mapped together with new curriculum standards so that you can have "air-tight" plans when you enter the classroom.

The initiatives revolve in cycles, usually every 1-3 years. You and your colleagues roll your eyes as the new one marches in. You know that This Year's Initiative is the same as Last Year's Initiative; the only difference is the language.

These initiatives are named with various proper and common nouns. Some "classics" include Maslow's Hierarchy and Bloom's Taxonomy. More recent evolutions include VAK (visual, auditory, kinesthetic) and Marzano's Nine Essential Instructional Strategies.

Why These Initiatives *Don't* Work

There is nothing wrong with any of these theories or strategies; I use most of them to create lessons and curriculum, myself. At best, however, they only address 50% of the equation! They only provide perspectives and tools for you, as the teacher, to deliver content.

They do not teach students how to process that content: how to consume it, analyze it, ask questions, or make decisions about it.

For example…

Maslow tells us that our students need to have their basic needs met in order to be in the "green zone" of learning. This is vital for teachers to know. But do we teach students how to deal with physical and emotional challenges that keep them from reaching their optimal state of learning?

Bloom taught us to recognize different levels of learning. But do students know about these different levels…let alone how to get into "high gear" learning?

Visual, Auditory, and Kinesthetic Learning Styles (VAK) are important for us, as teachers, to understand; we must be able to provide instruction and assess-

ments in a variety of modalities. However, VAK only confuses students; they can identify their preferred learning styles, but there is very little they can do about it. They have no control over the assignments and tests they are *required* to do.

Marzano's Nine Essential Instructional Strategies are filled with great strategies for teachers, such as encouraging teachers to use "nonlinguistic representations" (otherwise known as "symbols") to represent relationships.

But *students* should be taught that visuals are very powerful for the brain! They should be coached to create their own visuals, instead of always having visuals presented *to* them. Otherwise, they are simply memorizing symbols (low-gear learning) instead of creating their own associations (high-gear learning).

You Are Fighting Gravity!

You are swamped with strategies detailing what *you* should do, making you very overwhelmed. Every day, you try to do better, but you keep feeling less effective.

Is it any wonder?

Everything you have been taught – every college class, PD session, and magazine article – suggests that *you* do all of the work. Meanwhile, students are only learning how to follow directions by memorizing visuals, filling in the blanks on graphic organizers, and answering questions instead of *creating* them.

The Other 50% of the Equation

You will always feel like you are slogging uphill until your students are empowered to learn strategically. Learning and soft skills are the great differentiator because they put students in the driver's seat. They teach students how to learn, how to ask questions and navigate their way with high-level skills.

Soft skills teach students how to think forward and set their own goals, create their own purpose for learning, organize their papers and supplies, learn strategically, and monitor their progress along the way.

Notice that none of these skills is about *you* doing more work.

It is time for *students* to carry the weight of their own success! The best part is that they *want* this responsibility; they thrive on a good challenge and would love to be woken from their educational coma! (Just as I was!)

With learning and soft skills, they will have the tools to meet these challenges effectively and you will stop fighting gravity. Instead, you will become the encouraging coach and facilitator you envisioned when you chose this profession. It's a win-win for everyone!

Seize the day!

Susan

Two Ways to Raise
State & Standardized Test Scores

Research consistently confirms that there are *two* critical requirements for achieving optimal results on state and standardized testing:

1. **Teach the curriculum, not "to the test."** Teaching "to the test" – also known as "item teaching" – actually *lowers* test scores; it promotes only narrow, rigid thinking. [1,2] (It is directly opposed to #2 also.) Instead, students get better results when instruction is focused on the content *represented* on the test. This body of knowledge is typically known as your content standards.

   However, "teaching the curriculum" is completely ineffective if students don't have "cognitive flexibility"....

2. **Build cognitive flexibility with metacognitive strategies.**[3] If students do not have strategies for learning the content, well... they won't learn it! Obviously.

The National Research Council concludes that teaching students how to *ask questions* is the key to successful problem solving.[3] As you will notice, the "A" in SOAR® stands for "Ask questions." All metacognitive strategies presented in SOAR® use the process of "asking questions" as the primary strategy for learning new information.

Other strategies that have been research-validated to raise test performance include:

- **Promote goal-setting and monitoring.**[4,5] The "S" in SOAR® stands for "Set goals." Students will learn a simple, yet comprehensive, approach to thinking forward to create goals. SOAR® concludes with an "R" for "Record your progress," where students learn to monitor their goals.

- **Cultivate student reflection.**[6,7,8] SOAR® is built upon the understanding that metacognitive growth only happens through the process of reflection. *All* strategies are presented in a student-friendly manner that encourages self-reflection. Three (out of five) of the sections in this program are specifically centered around self-reflection: Section 1–*How Are You Smart?*, Section 2-*Set Goals*, and Section 5-*Record Your Progress*. Even Section 4-*Ask Questions* requires student reflection in order to create the questions to ask.

   In the SOAR® Multi-Media Teacher's Guide, all lessons begin with a Spiral Review class discussion and close with a class discussion review. "Reflection" very naturally becomes part of the culture with SOAR®.

State & Standardized Tests

- **Encourage self-evaluation of work.**[4,9,10] The most powerful element of "self-evaluation" in SOAR® is the Exit Presentation, which is the final assessment. For the Exit Presentation, students reflect on the content they've learned, provide *evidence* of their learning, and describe how this learning will be helpful in the workplace. The long-term impact of the Exit Presentation cannot be overstated!

- **Learn from mistakes.**[11,12] The most powerful strategy listed in Chapter 12, How to Take Tests, is to take time to review tests *after* they have been graded. There truly is no better way to learn than from our mistakes! The process does not improve the immediate test grade, but it will make an impact on future tests!

- **Teach how to take tests.**[13] Treat "tests" as another genre of literacy. Chapter 12, How to Take Tests, provides many tips on how to take a wide variety of tests. Some educators object to this, saying students must learn the *content*! Of course this is true and *genuine learning* is the primary object of SOAR®. However, if students are confused by various aspects of test-taking, their true content knowledge will not be reflected in their score either. It's in everyone's best interest for students to know how to navigate various types of tests.

<u>WARNING!</u>

"Metacognitive" strategies are not helpful if students don't know *how* and *when* to use them. This is the core problem of most "metacognitive" instruction. The skills are taught for one, isolated situation, but students do not know when to use that skill again. Or, they have learned so many different metacognitive skills, they can't remember all of them.

With SOAR®, we focus on the one, basic, core *strategy* of learning, which is to make connections. From there, we teach how to "ask questions" as the basic tactic for making learning connections. This simplification empowers students to use "metacognitive strategies" in a wide variety of situations…including on high-stakes tests!

Research Citations:

All citations from this article can be found at www.StudySkills.com/bonus-edu.

SOAR® Learning & Soft Skills
Covers 100% of Common Core Anchor Standards!

Common Core Anchor Standard: Number & Description	SOAR® Content: Description & Page Number
CCSS.ELA-Literacy.CCRA.R.1 Read closely to determine what the text says explicitly and to make logical inferences from it; cite specific textual evidence when writing or speaking to support conclusions drawn from the text.	How to Read Textbooks & Nonfiction: p. 99-103 How to Write Papers: p.130-131
CCSS.ELA-Literacy.CCRA.R.2 Determine central ideas or themes of a text and analyze their development; summarize the key supporting details and ideas.	How to Read Textbooks & Nonfiction: p. 99-103
CCSS.ELA-Literacy.CCRA.R.3 Analyze how and why individuals, events, or ideas develop and interact over the course of a text.	How to Read Textbooks & Nonfiction: p. 99-103
CCSS.ELA-Literacy.CCRA.R.4 Interpret words and phrases as they are used in a text, including determining technical, connotative, and figurative meanings, and analyze how specific word choices shape meaning or tone.	How to Study Vocabulary: p. 103 How to Use Language Resources:p. 143-144
CCSS.ELA-Literacy.CCRA.R.5 Analyze the structure of texts, including how specific sentences, paragraphs, and larger portions of the text (e.g., a section, chapter, scene, or stanza) relate to each other and the whole.	How to Read Textbooks & Nonfiction: p. 99-103
CCSS.ELA-Literacy.CCRA.R.6 Assess how point of view or purpose shapes the content and style of a text.	Listening & Comprehension Model: p. 89 How to Read Textbooks & Nonfiction: p. 100-102
CCSS.ELA-Literacy.CCRA.R.7 Integrate and evaluate content presented in diverse media and formats, including visually and quantitatively, as well as in words.	Listening & Comprehension Model: p. 89 How to Read Textbooks & Nonfiction: p. 99-103 How to Take & Study Notes: p. 105-113
CCSS.ELA-Literacy.CCRA.R.8 Delineate and evaluate the argument and specific claims in a text, including the validity of the reasoning as well as the relevance and sufficiency of the evidence.	Listening & Comprehension Model: p. 89 How to Do Internet Research & Verify Sources: p.126
CCSS.ELA-Literacy.CCRA.R.9 Analyze how two or more texts address similar themes or topics in order to build knowledge or to compare the approaches the authors take.	Listening & Comprehension Model: p. 89 How to Read Textbooks & Nonfiction: p. 99-103
CCSS.ELA-Literacy.CCRA.R.10 Read and comprehend complex literary and informational texts independently and proficiently.	How to Read Textbooks & Nonfiction: p. 99-103
CCSS.ELA-Literacy.CCRA.W.1 Write arguments to support claims in an analysis of substantive topics or texts using valid reasoning and relevant and sufficient evidence.	Writing & Speaking Model: p. 88 How to Write Papers: p. 124-136
CCSS.ELA-Literacy.CCRA.W.2 Write informative/explanatory texts to examine and convey complex ideas and information clearly and accurately through the effective selection, organization, and analysis of content.	Writing & Speaking Model: p. 88 How to Write Papers: p. 124-136
CCSS.ELA-Literacy.CCRA.W.3 Write narratives to develop real or imagined experiences or events using effective technique, well-chosen details, and well-structured event sequences.	Writing & Speaking Model: p. 88 How to Write Papers: p. 124-136
CCSS.ELA-Literacy.CCRA.W.4 Produce clear and coherent writing in which the development, organization, and style are appropriate to task, purpose, and audience.	Writing & Speaking Model: p. 88 How to Write Papers: p. 124-136
CCSS.ELA-Literacy.CCRA.W.5 Develop and strengthen writing as needed by planning, revising, editing, rewriting, or trying a new approach.	Writing & Speaking Model: p. 88 How to Write Papers: p. 124-136 Revising & Editing Checklist: p. 133
CCSS.ELA-Literacy.CCRA.W.6 Use technology, including the Internet, to produce and publish writing and to interact and collaborate with others.	How to Do Online Research & Verify Sources: p. 126 3-D Organizer e-Version: p. 136
CCSS.ELA-Literacy.CCRA.W.7 Conduct short as well as more sustained research projects based on focused questions, demonstrating understanding of the subject under investigation.	Writing & Speaking Model: p. 88 How to Write a Research Report: p. 126-136

CCSS.ELA-Literacy.CCRA.W.8 Gather relevant information from multiple print and digital sources, assess the credibility and accuracy of each source, and integrate the information while avoiding plagiarism.	Writing & Speaking Model: p. 88 How to Do Online Research & Verify Sources: p. 126 How to Write a Research Report: p. 126-136
CCSS.ELA-Literacy.CCRA.W.9 Draw evidence from literary or informational texts to support analysis, reflection, and research.	Writing & Speaking Model: p. 88 How to Write a Research Report: p. 126-136
CCSS.ELA-Literacy.CCRA.W.10 Write routinely over extended time frames (time for research, reflection, and revision) and shorter time frames (a single sitting or a day or two) for a range of tasks, purposes, and audiences.	How to Write Papers: p. 124-136 How to Write an Email: p. 136 Lesson Reviews: see MMTG
CCSS.ELA-Literacy.CCRA.SL.1 Prepare for and participate effectively in a range of conversations and collaborations with diverse partners, building on others' ideas and expressing their own clearly and persuasively.	Writing & Speaking Model: p. 88 Listening & Comprehnsion Model: p. 89 How to Work with Teachers & Peers: p. 90-98 Spiral Reviews & Daily Reviews: see MMTG
CCSS.ELA-Literacy.CCRA.SL.2 Integrate and evaluate information presented in diverse media and formats, including visually, quantitatively, and orally.	Listening & Comprehension Model: p. 89 How to Read Textbooks & Nonfiction: p. 99-103 How to Take & Study Notes: p. 105-113
CCSS.ELA-Literacy.CCRA.SL.3 Evaluate a speaker's point of view, reasoning, and use of evidence and rhetoric.	Listening & Comprehension Model: p. 89 How to Do Online Research & Verify Sources: p. 126
CCSS.ELA-Literacy.CCRA.SL.4 Present information, findings, and supporting evidence such that listeners can follow the line of reasoning and the organization, development, and style are appropriate to task, purpose, and audience.	Speaking & Writing Model: p. 88 How to Give a Presentation: p. 137-142 Spiral Review & Daily Review: see MMTG
CCSS.ELA-Literacy.CCRA.SL.5 Make strategic use of digital media and visual displays of data to express information and enhance understanding of presentations.	How to Give a Presentation: p. 137-142 How to Strategically Use: Visuals, Props, & Digital Media: p. 140 Exit Presentation: see MMTG
CCSS.ELA-Literacy.CCRA.SL.6 Adapt speech to a variety of contexts and communicative tasks, demonstrating command of formal English when indicated or appropriate.	Speaking & Writing Model: p. 88 How to Use Language Resources: p. 143-144 Spiral Review & Daily Review: see MMTG
CCSS.ELA-Literacy.CCRA.L.1 Demonstrate command of the conventions of standard English grammar and usage when writing or speaking.	How to Use Language Resources: p. 143-144 Capitilization, Punctuation, & Spelling: p. 143 Most Common Lanuage Errors: p. 143
CCSS.ELA-Literacy.CCRA.L.2 Demonstrate command of the conventions of standard English capitalization, punctuation, and spelling when writing.	How to Use Language Resources: p. 143-144 Most Common Lanuage Errors: p. 143
CCSS.ELA-Literacy.CCRA.L.3 Apply knowledge of language to understand how language functions in different contexts, to make effective choices for meaning or style, and to comprehend more fully when reading or listening.	What to Do When You Come to a Word You Don't Know: p. 103 How to Learn New Vocabulary Words: p. 103 How to Use Lanaguage Resources: p. 143-144
CCSS.ELA-Literacy.CCRA.L.4 Determine or clarify the meaning of unknown and multiple-meaning words and phrases by using context clues, analyzing meaningful word parts, and consulting general and specialized reference materials, as appropriate.	What to Do When You Come to a Word You Don't Know: p. 103 How to Learn New Vocabulary Words: p. 103 How to Use Lanaguage Resources: p. 143-144
CCSS.ELA-Literacy.CCRA.L.5 Demonstrate understanding of figurative language, word relationships, and nuances in word meanings.	How to Figure Out Figurative Language: p. 144
CCSS.ELA-Literacy.CCRA.L.6 Acquire and use accurately a range of general academic and domain-specific words and phrases sufficient for reading, writing, speaking, and listening at the college and career readiness level; demonstrate independence in gathering vocabulary knowledge when encountering an unknown term important to comprehension or expression.	What to Do When You Come to a Word You Don't Know: p. 103 How to Learn New Vocabulary Words: p. 103 Know Your Language!: p. 144 How to Use Lanaguage Resources: p. 143-144

SOAR® Learning & Soft Skills:
Teacher & Administrator FAQs

Answers to the following questions can be found at: www.StudySkills.com/bonus-edu.

Does the SOAR® Curriculum Fit My Needs?

What's included? Get more information about our Multi-Media Teacher's Guide, which includes 180+ done-for-you slides, assessments, and optional enrichment activities.

- **Common Core:** SOAR® covers 100% of Common Core College and Career Readiness Anchor Standards. See how to make this a strategic advantage for your students.
- **Response to Intervention (RTI):** SOAR® is commonly used as a Tier I and Tier II solution for RTI.
- **Special for Private Schools:** Top private schools use SOAR® as a *recruiting* tool! See how one of these schools makes it work in our video interview, "The Recruiting Power of Learning & Soft Skills."

Does SOAR® Work?

Research • Data/Proof • Guarantee

- **Raise GPAs by 1 Full Point!** See a video interview with the principal who saw these results and more in her school.
- **98% effective!** This rating was provided by an independent survey of teachers.
- **Research-based.** SOAR® is built on research-based best-practices in effective learning.
- **100% money-back guarantee!** If you don't get results, you can get your money back.

More details are provided at: www.StudySkills.com/bonus-edu.

FOR ADMINISTRATORS: "Where Do I Get Started?"

- **"Who will get this instruction?"** Determine the best grades, classes, or students.
- **"How can we fit it in our schedule?"** See the scheduling options other schools have used.
- **"What materials and supplies are needed?"** The recommended supplies are often less expensive than traditional school supplies.
- **"How can I get my staff on board without overwhelming them?"** Our Implementation Guide includes our best-practices for promoting staff-wide support. More details are available at: www.StudySkills.com/bonus-edu.

FOR TEACHERS: "How Do I Get Started?"

- **Pacing Guide:** See our video with suggestions for pacing instruction.
- **5-Step Curriculum Implementation Plan:** This plan can be used for all curriculum programs, not just SOAR®.
- **How to Become an Optimal Teacher, Even with a Million Mandates:** We know you are stretched to your maximum capacity. This video and article offer some long overdue feedback on the excellent work you are already doing…and some valuable insights to help you feel more effective. **BONUS:** The video includes time-saving tips and insights for increasing motivation while decreasing your workload!
- **How to Get Students in the "Green Zone" for Learning:** See a simple (and fun!) strategy to inspire powerful motivation in the classroom…one of our most popular video-articles!

Answers to the previous questions can be found at: www.StudySkills.com/bonus-edu.

Dear Student,

I struggled in school! K-12 was a serious challenge for me. I had no confidence. Frankly, I felt "stupid." But, my life changed when I figured out *how* to learn.

I went from struggling in K-12 to getting straight A's in college...and college was a lot easier! My confidence soared! I discovered that I wasn't "stupid" after all. Instead, I had the power to do anything I wanted to do!

However, one day, I was suddenly hit with a deep sense of anger. "Why didn't someone teach me how to learn *earlier*?!" I wondered in frustration. The strategies helping me get straight A's in college would have been just as helpful in middle and high school! I thought about the years of misery, the hundreds (or thousands?) of dismal hours of homework, and all of the tears shed in frustration. Realizing that those challenges could have been avoided so easily made the anger brew deeply.

I tried to tell myself there was no sense getting angry over the past. But this logic was not enough to erase the deep frustration. My heart and mind were engaged in a very intense wrestling match.

Suddenly, I had the most defining moment of my life. The inner turmoil settled right down.

No, I couldn't change the past. But I could change the future for others! In that moment, I knew that I had an obligation to future students to unlock the mysteries of learning. And that's what I've been doing ever since.

It turns out, these strategies are helpful for all students: if you already get straight A's, this book will show you how to do it with less stress. These strategies will continue to serve you in college and the workplace!

They will also help you earn good money. Employers list these skills as their "most needed." Yet they have a difficult time finding quality employees, even during a severe recession. Personally, I still use these skills. I used them to write this book and to build my business. I continue to use them every day at work and to manage my life and family at home.

If you use the information in this book to improve your life in any way, you will have made all of my frustration worthwhile. I hope you will seize this opportunity to change your life forever!

Most sincerely,

Susan

The "80/20" Power Strategy

I've got some good new and some bad news.

First, the bad news…
- 80% of your time only contributes to 20% of your happiness and success.
- 80% of the things you learn…will never be useful for you.
- 80% of the clothes in your closet are hardly ever worn.

But, the good news is…
- 20% of your time contributes to 80% of your happiness and success.
- 20% of the things you learn…will account for nearly all of your success in school, the workplace, and in life.
- 20% of the clothes in your closet are worn 80% of the time.

Why am I telling you this? Because this book contains the most critical 20% of skills you need to be successful in school…and in the workplace. I'm not making this up; this is not "my opinion."

It is a law of the universe. Like gravity.

It was first discovered in 1906 by an Italian economist named Vilfredo Pareto. Pareto noticed that 80% of the wealth in Italy was owned by 20% of the people. He then studied every other country – they were all the same: 20% of the people owned 80% of the wealth, *everywhere.*

It has since become a common rule in business: "80% of sales come from 20% of customers." But 80/20 applies to everything!

80/20 says that:
- 80% of points in sports are scored by 20% of the players.
- 80% of the traffic travels on 20% of the roads.
- 80% of your time is spent with 20% of your friends.

"80/20" is not always an 80/20 split—sometimes it's 70/30 or 90/10—but you will rarely see an even split between cause and effect.

80/20 Has a Direct Impact on Your Future

Hundreds of Fortune 500 CEOs were asked, "What makes people successful in the workplace?"

Their conclusion?

75% of a person's success in the workplace is determined by his or her ability to manage him-/herself and work with others. Only 25% of workplace success depends on technical knowledge.

Welcome, Students!

In other words, all of your time in school, from K to college, only affects 25% of your success. Yes, that 25% is critically important. But the remaining 75% is *even more* critical, and it's largely ignored in school. In the workplace, the "ability to manage oneself and work with others" is called "soft skills." In education, we call them "study skills" or "learning skills."

You are holding in your hands the most valuable 75% of your life! These skills will serve you in school and for the rest of your life! These are the same skills that transformed me from a life-long struggling student to a straight-A student in college. I didn't understand it at the time, but I was applying the 80/20 Principle to my own life. That's exactly *why* it worked!

That's not all!

Within the top 20%, there is always another "top 20%." For example:

- Of the 20% of the clothes that you wear most often, there is another 20% that you wear almost always. (Such as your favorite pair of jeans, or that ratty old sweatshirt you wear every night.)

- Of the 20% of people who own 80% of the wealth, 20% of those people own 80% of the 80%.

It's a bit crazy to wrap your brain around, but the patterns exist. Everywhere. And the same is true for this book. This book is the most valuable 75-80% of information you will ever learn.

But even within the pages of this book, there are some strategies that are even more helpful. For example, on page 100 there is a simple strategy for increasing your reading comprehension that is easily 80% more valuable than any of the other strategies in that chapter.

I call these "80/20 Power Strategies." They are marked with this icon:

Look for them and use them well! They are here to serve you and help you get better grades in school…in less time and with less stress. The solutions are so ridiculously simple, I don't want you to miss out on them!

SOAR® Lexicon

SOAR® is changing the way students think about learning! The SOAR® Lexicon below provides a preview of the approach and strategies that make us truly unique.

Strategic Learning™ – the process of using *strategies* to learn, avoiding the long, labor-intensive process of rehearsing and memorizing. Maximizing the strengths of the brain to learn as efficiently as possible.

Low-Gear Learning™ – the process of learning that is long, boring, and inefficient; usually involving repeated rehearsing and memorizing. The process of functioning in the lowest levels of the "Learning Pyramid."

High-Gear Learning™ – the process of learning that is fast, efficient, interesting, and utilizes strategy to bring out the brain's greatest potential. The process of functioning in the highest levels of the "Learning Pyramid."

Last-Minute Syndrome™ – the pain and frustration that comes from waiting until time is seriously limited before completing a task.

Think Forward™ – the mindset that cures Last-Minute Syndrome.

Take Ten™ – a simple, ten-minute routine that keeps students organized and saves hours of study time!

SOAR® Binder System™ – a student-friendly tool *and* process that eliminates lost papers and assignments.

Power Down™ – a highly impactful way to get more work done in less time; taking control of electronics so electronics do not control us. Small chunks of time cleared for "high-gear" learning, followed by "guilt-free" technology time.

Watch for these icons throughout the book:

	**80/20 Power Strategy™** This icon identifies strategies that provide big benefits for a small investment of time or effort. "Power strategies" are the cornerstone of SOAR®.
	**Teacher Talking Point** This icon suggests ways to ask good questions in class. Asking questions in class usually adds a valuable boost to your grades! (See Chapter 8 for more information.)
	**Students with Two Homes** This icon points out strategies that are exceptionally helpful for students who travel between more than one home regularly.

Welcome, Students!

Teachers:

Have you accessed your Multi-Media Teacher's Guide?

This book is provided with a license to use our Multi-Media Teacher's Guide including:

- 240+ Slides
- Four types of assesments
- Multi-Media extension activities
- Embeded videos
- Links to additional online content

Access to the Multi-Media Teacher's Guide is emailed to you at the time of purchase. If you have not recieved that email (check your "junk" folder), contact us at info@studyskills.com with:

- Your name
- School name/Distrcit name

We will confirm your license and respond with your access to the MMTG within 2-3 days.

How Are You Smart?

chapter 1

chapter 1

How Are You Smart?

chapter 1

How Are You Smart?

Many children and adults go through life feeling dumb, stupid, or simply "not smart" because of struggles they have had in school. Getting a good education is extremely important, but performance in school is not the only measure of a person's intelligence. You probably know many adults who did not get *good* grades in school yet are talented artists, businesspeople, tradesmen, etc.

Fortunately, many teachers are beginning to realize that intelligence is measured by more than students' performance on tests and written assignments. Over the last 20 years, Dr. Howard Gardner[1], Professor of Education at Harvard University, has been doing research on intelligence. He suggests that there are at least eight different types of human intelligence:

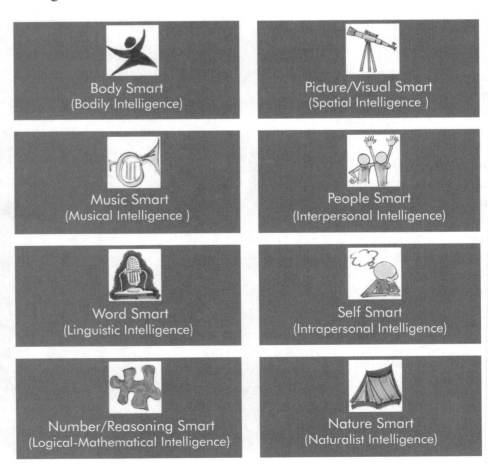

Body Smart
(Bodily Intelligence)

Picture/Visual Smart
(Spatial Intelligence)

Music Smart
(Musical Intelligence)

People Smart
(Interpersonal Intelligence)

Word Smart
(Linguistic Intelligence)

Self Smart
(Intrapersonal Intelligence)

Number/Reasoning Smart
(Logical-Mathematical Intelligence)

Nature Smart
(Naturalist Intelligence)

"Why Are These Intelligences Important?"

Schools traditionally measure students' abilities in *only* two intelligences: Number/Reasoning and Word Smarts. While these intelligences are important, they are not the only proof of a person's ability.

For example, I once had a student who struggled with reading, writing, and math (traditional schoolwork). However, he had an amazing ability to build objects and machines from scrap materials. He drew complex diagrams. He could instantly determine how anything mechanical worked. Many teachers viewed him as a "slow learner," but he simply struggled in two areas of intelligence (Word Smart and Number/Reasoning Smart). He had the potential to become a successful mechanic or industrial engineer, among other things.

Too many people – students and adults – struggle because they lack confidence in their abilities. They often think, "I may be a good artist, but I'm not smart," or, "I may be good at repairing things, but I'm not intelligent!" It is unfortunate that a great actor or comedian may not view his talent as a form of intelligence….each and every person is smart! Even a person who has a cognitive disability is likely gifted in some areas (interpersonal intelligence, for example).

Before the rest of this book can be helpful, you must believe in yourself *and* have confidence that you do have talents. If you have experienced problems in school, you simply have not yet been given the tools to break down the wall. Sections two through five of this book provide those tools. In the meantime, the following two pages encourage you to identify some of your natural strengths and the various ways that you are intelligent. (You can have strengths in many different areas of intelligence.)

Everyone has his or her own special talents…find yours and develop confidence in your own *smart self.*

What Is Your Super Power?

Your Super Power is the one thing you do better than 95% of the population! It's much more specific than a "type" of intelligence. It's a very special gift, but it's difficult for you to see because it comes so naturally to you.

Learn more about finding your Super Power at: www.StudySkills.com/bonus-edu.

KlektaDarya/Shutterstock

---

[1] Gardner, Howard. Intelligences Reframed: Multiple Intelligences for the 21st Century. New York: Basic Books, 1999.

How Are You Smart?

Do you enjoy, or feel talented in, any of the following activities?
Take this quiz and check all that apply:

Check:		
	Artistic projects such as drawing, painting, crafting, etc.	
	Helping/caring for other people (e.g., children, senior citizens)	
	Singing, composing, or playing a musical instrument	
	Completing math or logic problems	
	Journaling, meditating, or reflecting on thoughts and feelings	
	Building, creating, or fixing things	
	Working or playing outdoors	
	Speaking in front of large groups	
	Sports, dance, or performing arts	
	Daydreaming or picturing possibilities for yourself	
	Figuring out how things work	
	Decorating or arranging rooms	
	Listening to music to adjust your mood	
	Communicating with others or working effectively with a team	
	Setting and accomplishing goals for yourself	
	Working with animals and/or plants	
	Conversing with others, or telling jokes or stories	
	Humming or whistling while you work on other tasks	
	Classifying or organizing objects	
	Hunting, camping, or hiking	
	Completing tasks on the computer or playing video games	
	Making people feel comfortable	
	Reading maps	
	Learning or speaking foreign languages	

How Are You Smart? quiz format is adapted from SuperCamp®.

Would you describe yourself as:

Check:		
	Athletic	
	An enthusiastic reader or writer	
	A problem-solver	
	Musical	
	Visual	
	Friendly or patient with others	
	Nature lover	
	Spiritual, thoughtful, or insightful	
	Good with numbers	
	Having a sense of rhythm	
	Active	
	Sensitive to sounds, tones, or accents	
	Creative	
	Self-disciplined or independent	
	A "referee" with your friends and/or family	
	Animal lover	

Scoring

To identify your strongest "smarts," match the icon at the end of each checked item (from both pages) with the corresponding columns below. Create a bar graph of your results by shading in one box for every quiz item that has been checked, beginning at the bottom of each column.

How Are You Smart?

Math	Visual	Word	Music	People	Self	Body	Nature

You may have found interests and strengths in several different areas. Hopefully you are beginning to get a sense of each intelligence and what it means. The following pages provide more details:

Body Smart (Bodily-Kinesthetic Intelligence)

People who are gifted in this area generally enjoy sports, dance, or other areas of physical fitness. They are often referred to as "active" because they love to move! They learn best through movement and hands-on activities.

People in careers that use this intelligence include:
Craftspeople, physical/occupational therapists, surgeons, inventors, professional athletes, actors, farmers, dancers

Music Smart (Musical/Rhythmic Intelligence)

You do not have to be a gifted singer, composer, or instrument player to have talent in this area. You may enjoy music or have a strong sense of rhythm. You may learn best through songs, patterns, rhythms, and other forms of musical expression or find yourself frequently tapping or dancing to music.

People in careers that use this intelligence include:
Composers, song-writers, sound technicians, disc jockeys, instrument makers, music teachers, band directors

Word Smart (Linguistic Intelligence)

Word Smart people are often good at reading, writing, speaking, or a combination of the three. They may enjoy reading and written expression, or find they are good at telling jokes and stories or speaking in front of others. They may also have an interest in foreign languages. Some people may be very gifted in one area of Linguistic Intelligence, such as conversation skills, but struggle with another area, such as writing.

People in careers that use this intelligence include:
Salespeople, journalists/writers, editors, librarians, therapists, speech therapists, lawyers, interpreters

Number/Reasoning Smart (Logical/Mathematical Intelligence)

People with talents in this area are generally good math students. They are good at solving problems and puzzles with numbers or logic. Some are excellent at computing numbers in their head, estimating, or making conversions (e.g., in recipes). They may enjoy organizing, budgeting, or creating patterns.

People in careers that use this intelligence include:
Engineers, computer technicians/programmers, accountants, mathematicians, researchers, statisticians, financial analysts, professional organizers, physicians

Picture/Visual Smart (Spatial Intelligence)

While you don't have to be gifted in Picture Smarts to be called "creative," this is the term that is most often associated with individuals talented in Spatial Intelligence. People with strengths in this area are likely to be good at following or creating maps, noticing patterns, or assembling projects and puzzles. "Artistic" or "crafty" people are also gifted in Spatial Intelligence.

People in careers that use this intelligence include:
Graphic artists, interior designers, architects, engineers, photographers, videographers, inventors, drafters, builders, surveyors, urban planners

People Smart (Interpersonal Intelligence)

"People Smart" refers to the skills required to develop relationships with others. Individuals gifted in this intelligence often work very well on teams. They are skilled at making people feel comfortable in their presence. They usually enjoy helping others and may be good at resolving conflicts among family members and friends. Some People Smart individuals are very social and outgoing, while others may be reserved and shy. Either way, they are usually regarded as "nice" people.

People in careers that use this intelligence include:
Teachers, nurses, physicians, medical assistants, politicians, sales people, counselors/psychologists, mediators, consultants, business administrators (management), human resources

Self Smart (Intrapersonal Intelligence)

How well do you know yourself? If you are a reflective thinker, have a clear concept of your values and beliefs, or have a sense of spirituality or greater purpose, you are probably very Self Smart. Self Smart individuals have a strong concept of what they want in life, so they are likely to be very focused, self-disciplined, and independent. This intelligence usually develops with age and maturity.

People in careers that use this intelligence include:
Writers, entrepreneurs/self-employed, spiritual leaders, counselors/therapists, leaders, researchers

Nature Smart (Naturalist Intelligence)

"Nature Smart" people are inclined to be outdoors. They usually have a strong appreciation for the environment and respect for the beauty of nature. They are interested in plants, animals, or other natural resources and choose activities such as hiking, camping, hunting, stargazing, swimming, scuba diving, etc. as hobbies.

People in careers that use this intelligence include:
Meteorologists, park rangers, photojournalists, biologists, botanists, zoologists, veterinarians, anthropologists, sailors, astronomers

Intelligences + Soft Skills = Lifetime Success

I hope you have uncovered some hidden gems about your intelligence, or at least learned a little more about yourself. You have to recognize your talents in order to be motivated in school and in life. This internal motivation will make the strategies that follow even easier to use.

This book is designed to help you now and for the rest of your life. You will learn how to manage time, organize papers, and learn efficiently. These skills will help you get better grades now *and* earn more money in the workplace.

How Are You Smart?

-Summary-

1   **Everyone is intelligent!** There are at least eight different domains of intelligence, but schoolwork typically assesses only two types of intelligence: Math and Word Smarts.

2   **There are careers suited to every type of intelligence.** Even if Math and Word Smarts are not your top talents, you will be able to find a career that fits your natural gifts. In the meantime, try to sign up for elective classes and extracurricular activities that match your natural aptitudes.

3   **In order to be motivated in school and in life, you must recognize your intelligences and believe in your abilities.** When you feel good about yourself, you will soon discover that you can accomplish anything you set your mind to.

4   **Regardless of what your strongest intelligences are, it is important to get a good education.** This book offers tips and strategies to help *all* students make school and homework easier.

Set goals

section

2

Set goals

Check all statements below that apply to you:

_____ Do you feel that your homework takes longer than it should?

_____ Would you like to earn better grades while still having time for extracurricular activities and socializing?

_____ Do you ever forget what you have for homework?

_____ Do you ever forget certain books, notebooks, or folders at school that you need for homework?

_____ Are you tired of being nagged by your parents about homework and studying?

You will find solutions to these problems, and much more, in this section.

> The reason most people never reach their goals is that they don't define them or ever seriously consider them as believable or achievable.
>
> Winners can tell you where they are going, what they plan to do along the way, and who will be sharing the adventure with them.
>
> - Denis Watley

The first step towards getting better grades in less time is to decide exactly what you want by setting goals. The process of creating a goal is much like planning a trip: you must have a destination and a plan for how you will get there. The process of setting goals helps you focus on your desired achievements, minimize distractions, and identify time-saving steps along your way.

The process of setting a goal is much like planning a trip: you must have a destination and a plan for how you will get there.

The "map" in this book will guide you through a specific process for setting and achieving goals. After completing this process, you will discover the important parts of identifying and reaching your goals. However, you probably will not need to be as thorough in the future. After completing this process once, you will have the awareness and skills you need to achieve anything you want!

The Set Goals section of this book is broken down into the following three steps:

Establish your priorities.

   Identify your goals.

      Schedule time to take action.

These steps are highlighted at the beginning of each chapter to remind you how all of the components fit together.

chapter 2
Establish Your Priorities
Identify Your Goals
Schedule Time to Take Action

The first step to setting goals is to know your priorities. Priorities are the things most important to you. Happy, successful people will tell you that the key to happiness is making decisions according to your priorities, minimizing time and energy-wasters in their lives. You must know your most important priorities so you can create meaningful goals. Your priorities also help you *choose* how to spend your time. Otherwise, you will simply react to everything that comes your way.

Making Time for School and "Fun Stuff"

Find a good balance. School is important and should be a top priority, but "fun stuff" is just as important. In this chapter, you will learn how to balance everything you *have* to do with everything you *want* to do!

The pictures on the next page illustrate an important concept about prioritizing your time. Can you figure out what that concept is?

"What Can a Jar Teach Us About Prioritizing?"

1 This jar represents one day, 24 hours — no more, no less.

2 As you know, a day fills up fast. So does the jar.

Is this jar full?

There is no more room for rocks, but….

3 …there is plenty of room for pebbles.

Is it full yet?

There is not much more room for pebbles, but….

4 …there is, of course, room for a lot of water.

Is it full now?

It certainly is!

Rock, pebble, and water analogy adapted from: Covey, Sean. <u>The 7 Habits of Highly Effective Teens</u>. Salt Lake City, UT: Franklin Covey Co., 2000.

..."So, What's the Point?"

> ...That we have a lot of "big" things and "little" things to do in one day?

> ...That we can fit a lot into one day?

Both of these observations are partially correct, but there is more to it. The rock, pebble, and water analogy shows us that the *order* in which the items were added to the jar is critical. If we placed the pebbles in the jar first, there would be no space for rocks.

The jar is like your time. The big rocks automatically made room for pebbles and water; you can automatically make room for "fun stuff." Simply take care of your big priorities first.

"How Can This Help Me Manage My Time?"

As sure as a law of physics, homework that is started at 4:00 p.m. will get done faster than homework that is started at 8:00 p.m.

When you take care of your top priorities (big rocks) first, you automatically have space in your life for the things you *want* to do. For example, if you come home from school and start homework within a half-hour, you are taking care of a "rock" priority first. The sooner you start homework, the more fresh and efficient you will be. It is also very motivating to have a few free hours each evening. This free time often encourages you to stay focused and work more quickly. The later it gets, the more anxiety kicks in to slow you down.

Obviously, the faster you do homework, the more free time you will have.

But that's not all...

Your free time is *much* more enjoyable when your homework is done. It's no fun to have the burden of homework hanging over your head all evening.

"How Do I Determine My Priorities?"

The next two pages will guide you through the process of exploring your priorities. You will begin by reflecting on *how* you spend your time vs. how you *want* to spend your time. Then you will sort your list into different priorities. The priority categories are listed here:

Rock Priorities

Your rock priorities are the things you have to do. You have to go to school, do homework, help around the house, sleep, etc. These things usually have significant consequences if not done. Such consequences include, but are not limited to, getting bad grades, flunking a class, being grounded, and being too tired to function properly.

strelov/Shutterstock

Pebble Priorities

Pebble priorities are the things that you really enjoy and want to spend more time doing. Some examples may include sports, band, other extracurricular activities at school, a part-time job, a hobby, and more time to socialize with friends. Your pebble priorities are the "spice" in your life…the things that provide you with a satisfying sense of enjoyment. These priorities are "smaller" because they do not have as many consequences if not done; **however, smaller does not mean less significant.** You need to have a smart balance between rock and pebble priorities to lead a healthy life and maintain motivation for your rock priorities.

QiuJu Song/ Shutterstock

Water Priorities

Water priorities are "If I get to them, great. If not, oh well!" priorities. These are the little things that you enjoy doing, but do not necessarily need to schedule into your day, such as playing video games, watching TV, etc. It can sometimes be hard to distinguish between pebble and water priorities. If you are undecided about which category something belongs in, your indecision is a good sign that the task belongs in the "water" category. Water priorities will have less significance than either rock or pebble priorities if not done.

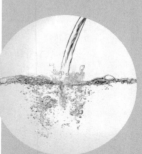

DSBfoto/Shutterstock

How Do You Spend Your Time?

In the chart below, make a list of everything you <u>like</u> to do and <u>have</u> to do with your time. Include school, homework, free-time activities, chores, and religious events (e.g. attending church/synagogue) if applicable. Also record how much time you spend on each activity per week. Finally, make a list of things you would like to have more time to do.

How I Spend My Time:	Average Hours per Day:	Amount of Time per Week:

Things I Would Like to Have More Time to Do:	Desired Hours per Day:	Desired Amount of Time per Week:

What Are Your Priorities?

Use the "How Do You Spend Your Time?" list from the previous page to determine your rock, pebble, and water priorities.

strelov/Shutterstock

My "Rock" Priorities Are:
(Things you <u>have</u> to do, such as school, homework, chores, family responsibilities, church/synagogue, etc.)

_____

_____

_____

_____

_____

My "Pebble" Priorities Are:
(Things you <u>enjoy</u> doing and which you want to make time for such as sports, friends, specific TV shows, etc.)

_____

_____

_____

_____

QiuJu Song/ Shutterstock

_____

_____

_____

_____

DSBfoto/Shutterstock

My "Water" Priorities Are:
("Filler time:" Things you enjoy doing but do not feel the need to schedule, such as watching general TV shows, texting friends, etc.)

_____

_____

_____

_____

_____

_____

_____

_____

chapter 3

Establish Your Priorities

Identify Your Goals

Schedule Time to Take Action

Now that you have sorted your priorities, you can set your goals. Maybe you would like to get better grades, have more free time, or make the varsity basketball team. Anything is possible if you create a plan. The plan begins with the final destination: your goals.

Helpful Hint

One of your priorities should benefit your health. Examples include goals related to sports, physical fitness, nutrition, and healthy sleep.

Step 1: Identify Your Top Priorities

Choose three significant priorities from the previous page and record them below. To maintain a healthy balance in your life, make sure at least one priority is for school or homework (which should be listed as a rock priority), and one priority is from your pebble category. The third priority can be from either the rock or pebble category.

 priority 1 Rock Priority—School/Homework

_____

 priority 2 Pebble Priority

_____

 priority 3 Rock or Pebble Priority

_____

Step 2: Turn Your Priorities Into Goals

Turn your priorities from the previous page into goals by answering the following questions:

| priority 1 | Rock Priority—School/Homework
How do you want to improve in this part of your life?
What would you like to accomplish? |

_____

_____

_____

_____

| priority 2 | Pebble Priority
How do you want to improve in this part of your life?
What would you like to accomplish? |

_____

_____

_____

_____

| priority 3 | Rock or Pebble Priority
How do you want to improve in this part of your life?
What would you like to accomplish? |

_____

_____

_____

_____

Step 3: Create a Plan for Achieving Your Goals

"Big" goals cannot be accomplished in one day; they usually require many steps over a long period of time. So you must do more than just create goals; you have to create a plan for *achieving* them by breaking them into smaller, manageable steps. On page 48, you will make a specific list of all the things you need to do in order to achieve the three goals you just described.

Follow the steps to create an effective plan for achieving your objectives:

 step 1
Write each goal at the top of the three ladders on page 48.

Imagine your goals are at the top of a ladder…and each step on the ladder is a step towards your goal.

 step 2
Think about every little step you will need to take to reach your goal. List the steps under each specific goal.

Be specific. You must be able to physically do each task. You must be able to close your eyes and actually visualize yourself doing the task. For example, you cannot see yourself getting good grades, but you can see yourself reviewing your notes every night for 20 minutes.

step 3
See the sample list of goals on page 47 to help you identify appropriate, specific actions.

Note that one of the lists includes more steps than others. You will find some goals require many steps and others require just a few.

Also, note that some goals will rely on other goals. For example, in order to accomplish the third goal on page 47, this person will rely on steps from the first goal.

Reaching for a goal is like climbing a ladder… you go one step at a time.

GOAL

Raise every grade by one letter this quarter.

Action

Plan my week on Sundays.

(See Chapter 7.)

Action

Use my planner every day.

Action

Spend 10 min. at the end of each day reviewing notes.

Action

Keep all of my papers organized in a SOAR® Binder.
(See Chapter 5.)

Action

Go to math tutoring during lunch once a week.

Action

Turn in all of my homework.

Action

GOAL

Stay in shape so I can make the varsity basketball team.

Action

Shoot hoops for 20 minutes, 3 days a week.

Action

Join a recreational league over the summer.

Action

Run for 20 minutes, 2-3 times per week.

Action

Lift weights when coach opens up the gym after school.

Action

Action

Action

GOAL

Spend more time with friends while getting good grades.

Action

Do everything listed under the first goal.

Action

Do as much homework in school as possible.

Action

Do h.w. as soon as I get home so I have more time at night.

Action

Ask my parents for rides (or the car) at the beg. of the week or ASAP.

Action

Action

Action

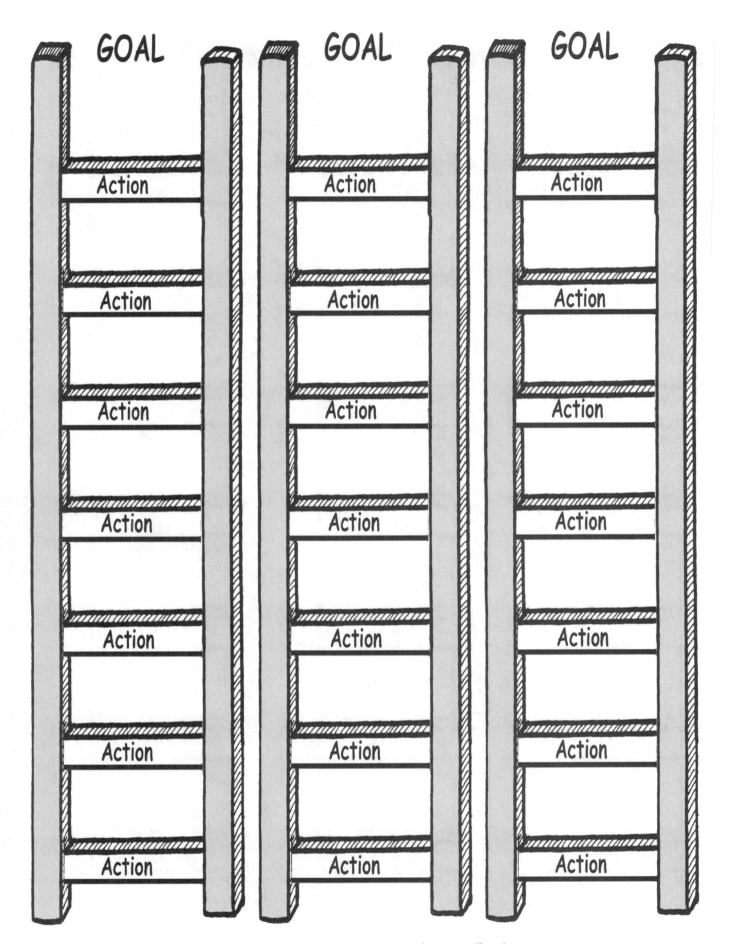

chapter 4

Establish Your Priorities

Identify Your Goals

Schedule Time to Take Action

Now that you have identified a few major goals and the actions needed to achieve those goals, you need to make a plan for reaching them.

The Time Tool

The best tool for scheduling time and managing responsibilities is an academic planner. You have a lot to juggle: school, homework, family, and social responsibilities. You may likely have after-school sports, activities, or a part-time job. Each of these responsibilities requires planning, updating, and tracking dates, times, and assignments. A planner is a living tool that serves as your base for keeping track of responsibilities, evaluating priorities, and making decisions about how to spend your time.

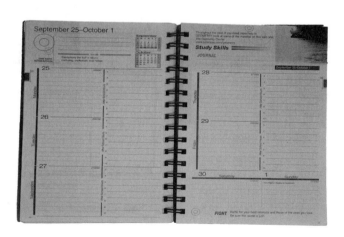

A planner is a living tool that serves as your base for evaluating priorities, keeping track of responsibilities, and making decisions about how to spend your time.

Planners Are Essential for Everyone

If you think a planner will not work for you, then you probably:

> Planners don't work for me!

> I do just fine without a planner!

a) have not been using the right planner.
b) have not used a planner correctly.
c) have not made using a planner a habit.
d) some or all of the above.

Have you ever forgotten an assignment or book for homework? To study for a test? If so, you are not doing as well as you could be. A planner reduces anxiety because it helps you keep track of what needs to be done. It gives you a sense of control.

Are you more of a last minute person? A planner helps you do exactly what you are probably not comfortable doing…planning ahead to avoid last-minute headaches.

> A planner is absolutely necessary to balance with your priorities and maximize your time!

Anchor Points: When and How to Use a Planner

There are several different times you should use your planner throughout the week. I call these "anchor points" because they will help you navigate the best path towards successful use of a planner:

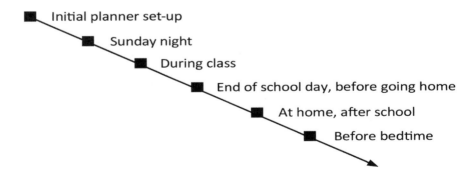

- Initial planner set-up
- Sunday night
- During class
- End of school day, before going home
- At home, after school
- Before bedtime

It may take 2-3 weeks before you get into a groove with a planner, but do not give up! It will take a few pages to describe some simple tips, but it will not take very long to make this tool work for you!

Initial Planner Set-Up

Get a binder clip and use it! The binder clip will let you open your planner to the current page *instantly*. You are much more likely to use your planner if you do not have to flip through dozens of pages every time you need to write something down. (Paper clips are not good because they slip off easily.)

Get phone numbers of responsible classmates; write them in the back of your planner. When you have questions about an assignment, you can text or call someone.

Are there special websites or specific URLs you will need to access class information? Write this information in the back of your planner, or in a special "notes" section, depending on your planner. This information should always be at your fingertips.

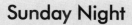

Sunday Night

Spend ten minutes on Sundays preparing for the week. Pull out your planner. Write down your goals for the week, sports practices, project due dates, test dates, work schedules, etc. Highlight test or project due dates and then consider, "What do I have the night before?" If you have a basketball game the night before a big test, then you need to plan on spending extra time studying two nights before the test.

Do you feel like your parents nag you too much? Would you like them to stop? Ask your parents what their schedules are for the week. Ask if they have anything planned for you, such as a doctor's appointment or birthday dinner for your great-aunt. Let them know about your upcoming week, too.

Parents "nag" because they want to be sure you get your homework done, that you get good grades, etc. They want what is best for you! If *you* take the initiative to tell your parents about your schedule and plans, they will know that you have things under control. When parents know you have things under control, they don't *need* to nag.

Hundreds of parents and students have said that these few minutes of planning together have a huge impact! It really does work! Life becomes much less chaotic, and their relationships with each other improve.

Students with Two Homes

If your parents/guardians live in two different homes, the Sunday Night Conference is a critical strategy for you to use with both parents.

Take a few minutes to speak with each parent. If possible, have both parents on the phone with you. Talk to them about your schedule for the week. Make sure they both know about any practices you have after school, big tests, or projects that you have coming up. Double-check when you will visit the other parent, who will be picking you up from soccer practice, etc.

This conference is the single best thing you can do for yourself when you call two places "home."

During Class

Keep a pen or mechanical pencil in the rings of your planner so you can *instantly* write notes. If you have to dig through your bag to find a pen or pencil, you won't use your planner.

Keep your planner accessible. The best place to keep your planner is on your desk. If that's not possible, keep it on top of the rest of your belongings, under the desk. Once again, you are more likely to use a planner if you do not have to dig for it.

Record your homework as it is assigned in class. Also make notes of the books you will need to take home. Do not wait until the end of the day to write down assignments, because you are likely to record the *wrong* assignment or not record anything at all.

End of School Day, Before Going Home

Plan your homework time. Sometime before you go home from school (perhaps in the final moments of your last class or on the bus), take a few seconds to plan when you will work on homework that evening. Review your planner notes and write down how much time you will need for each assignment so you can appropriately plan how much time you will need.

Check your planner before you go home; be sure you have all of the books you need. This will take no more than five seconds if you have the current page marked with a binder clip and your planner is easily accessible in your arms or book bag.

Time-Saving Tip

Minimize homework time by using every second in school:

- Pay attention in class so you don't have to relearn everything when you sit down to do homework.
- During the moments you are waiting in class, open your binder and reread your notes from all of your classes. A few minutes in class saves a lot of study time at home!

At Home, After School

Stick to your schedule! Share it with your parents so that they know you have everything under control. If something comes up, or you simply get off track, don't fret. Get back on track by taking care of your "rock" priorities first.

Power down. Stay on schedule by turning off all electronics during homework time. Using electronics will only delay your progress. Turn off cell phones (no calls or text-messages...save them for later), turn off the TV, music, computer, and tablets. If you need to use a computer to do your work, turn off all notices from social media, email, etc. Consider using a program that limits your access to distracting apps. (See "How to Control Computer Distractions" at www. StudySkills. com/bonus-edu.) Turning everything off may not sound very fun, but it will help you get your homework done much quicker. Do yourself a favor: avoid distractions, get homework done quickly, then enjoy TV, music, the computer/tablet, and texting later. (It's all about priorities!)

Time-Saving Tip

Use a timer to help you stay focused while working on homework. Set the timer for the amount of time you think a homework assignment should take, and then work to "beat the clock." Of course, the point is not to rush your work, but to stay focused and avoid distractions.

Before Bedtime

Check your planner one last time. Did you get all forms signed? Is all of your homework in your bag? Do you have your lunch money? Is there anything else you needed to take care of? This last check will make your mornings much less chaotic.

Get everything you need for the next day in your bag and placed by the door before you go to bed. This simple habit reduces morning craziness. You will also feel much more prepared when you get to school the next day.

Keeping a Good Balance

Record everything in your planner. Use it to track appointments, notes about family events, and goals for other areas of your life.

For Example…

A sample planner page is on page 55.

The items in bold show what this student planned at the beginning of the week. Notice that one of her weekly goals was to shoot hoops and run three days this week. So, she plugged those items into her planner on Monday, Tuesday, and Thursday. She has a TV program on Monday night that she does not want to miss, so she wrote that down, too. She also recorded time to review her notes every day. She is even reviewing her notes on Friday afternoon, but she is giving herself a break from all other homework Friday night.

On Monday, she recorded her homework in each class, as it was assigned. In 8th hour, she spent two minutes figuring out when she would do her homework that night. Her schedule may get thrown off a bit, but if it does, she still has a structure to follow to get back on track. Even with a few setbacks, she's well on her way towards achieving her third goal: having at least two hours of homework-free time every night. She'll likely have a lot more free time, too!

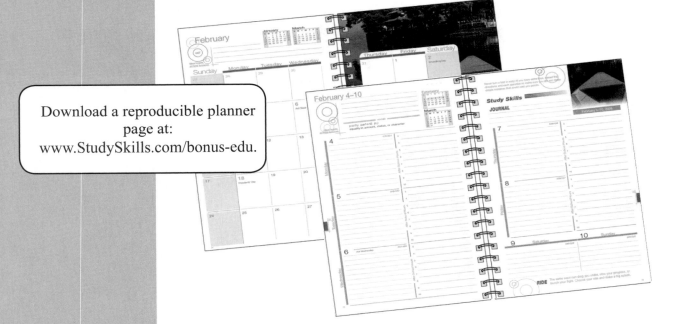

Download a reproducible planner page at:
www.StudySkills.com/bonus-edu.

A good planner should include a monthly *and* weekly layout for long-term and short-term planning.

Planner images courtesy of www.actionagendas.com.

Sept	3 Monday	4 Tuesday	5 Wednesday	6 Thursday	7 Friday	8 Saturday
1st hour	Page 161 # 2-20 all					- Get homework done this morning (2 hours?)
2nd hour	None					
3rd hour	Get Permission Slip Signed					
4th hour	None					
5th hour						
6th hour	Study for Chapter 4 Test on Thurs.					**9 Sunday**
7th hour	Read section 5.2. Questions pg. 109			Science test today		Grandma's b-day
Other	Math book Science book Language Arts book					lunch 1 p.m.
3 p.m.	Snack	Movie Club Mtg. Snack	Snack	Snack	Snack	**Weekly Goals**
4 p.m.	Shoot hoops & run	Shoot hoops & run	Review all notes for 15 minutes/ Do Math	Shoot hoops & run	Review all notes for 15 minutes	- Shoot hoops and run three days this week
5 p.m.	Review all notes for 15 minutes/ Do Math	Review all notes for 15 minutes/ Do Math	Study 15 min. for Science test	Review all notes for 15 minutes/ Do Math	No other homework tonight!	- Review notes every day
6 p.m.	Study Science 15 min. L. Arts HW (1 hr)	Study 20 min. for Science test				
7 p.m.					Football game	- Have at least two hours of homework-free time every evening!
8 p.m.	Watch TV Show at 8:30					
9-10 p.m.	10:30 Read in bed/Sleep	10:30 Read in bed/Sleep	10:30 Read in bed/Sleep	10:30 Read in bed/ Sleep		

Selecting a Planner

Most planners on the market are more confusing than they are helpful! There are several things to consider when looking for a planner:

An effective planner for middle school, high school, and college will have:

❶ A page to view an entire month at once, PLUS

❷ One week of planning space per page, or per two-page spread. This means that you should be able to see seven days without having to turn a page.

❸ Space to record weekly goals is very helpful, but not necessary.

A planner should always be easy to carry. The easier it is to transport, the more likely you are to use it.

Bulky planners are too impractical to carry around and keep accessible.

Problem planners have:

❶ A bulky binder, leather, or fabric cover. These planners are too big to carry around easily. If it is inconvenient to carry a planner, you simply will not use it.

❷ Only one day of planning space per page; this layout makes weekly planning impossible.

Some Cautions About Using Mobile Phones

I used to completely discourage the use of mobile phones as "planners" for two reasons: first, it was difficult to enter information in them. Second, it was challenging to see several dates at one time, making weekly planning impossible. However, smart phones are changing the game enough to make me reconsider.

The single best advantage to using a smart phone is that it is rarely out of your reach. Using a phone also allows you to program alarms and SMS messages as reminders, which can be very useful for managing schoolwork and after-school activities.

However, there are important guidelines to follow if you will use your phone as your planner:

① **Does your school allow the use of phones in class?** If not, stick with a traditional planner.

② **All of the guidelines from this chapter still apply:** you should still review your week on Sunday evening, coordinate with your family, record homework as it is assigned in class, check your list of assignments before you leave school at the end of the day, etc.

③ **Alarms and SMS reminders should *only* be used as "back-up" reminders.** You should review your calendar and assignment list weekly and daily to stay aware of your responsibilities. This process prevents them from becoming "last-minute" issues, which will eat up a lot of your extra time and energy.

rvlsoft/Shutterstock

Planners: A Life-long Tool

Developing the habit of using a planner does take some effort, but the payoff is well worth it!

- Schoolwork will be easier.
- Your grades will automatically improve.
- Your stress level will decrease because *you* will be in control.
- Learning these skills now will make life in the "real world" much easier and lead to great success!

Set goals
-Summary-

1 **Setting goals is an essential element of success.** If you never set a destination, you'll never get there.

2 **Always know your priorities.** Knowing what is most important in your life helps you make critical decisions about how to spend your time. Your priorities help you reach your goals.

3 **Rank your priorities.** Make room for "fun stuff" by taking care of your "big rocks," first.

4 **Schedule time to take action.** The key to accomplishing your goals is to plan for action.

Organize

section

3

Organize

Check all statements below that apply to you:

_____ Have you ever brought the wrong notebook or folder to class or home for homework?

_____ Have you ever misplaced a homework assignment that you know you did?

_____ When you look inside your bag and locker, is there a sea of randomly stashed papers staring back at you?

_____ Do you have a hard time keeping your room neat and organized?

_____ Do you ever feel rushed and frustrated getting ready for school?

You will find solutions to these problems, and much more, in the following section.

> For every minute spent organizing, an hour is earned.

What Is the Cost of Disorganization?

Disorganization costs valuable time and energy. It can steal points from your grades and cost a lot of money.

A moderately disorganized person loses about two hours every day due to disorder. If your income is $100,000 per year, based on a 40-hour work week, that adds up to $25,000 lost every year!

Find out *exactly* what disorganization costs you with my "Cost of Disorganization" calculator at www.StudySkills.com/bonus-edu.

Organization is the vital foundation for success in school and the workplace. Even if you are not naturally organized, these skills can be learned. Certainly, some people will find organizing easier than others. But, *anyone* can learn strategies to create order in his or her life.

As always, the goal of this section is to share *easy* strategies. Strategies that require a short amount of time to do but save a lot of time and hassle. In this section, you will learn about a great system for organizing all of your papers and notebooks for school. It is simple, cheap, and easy to use. You will also learn some tips for keeping your room, book bag, and locker in neat, functional order. Finally, you will review many different ways to organize your time by developing simple routines.

The more you organize, the more you simplify your life. The more you simplify your life, the more efficient you become. The more efficient you are, the more time you have for fun stuff!

chapter 5
Organize Your Papers
Organize Your Space
Organize Your Time

Managing papers, folders, and notebooks is one of the most common challenges for students. As a student you are constantly moving, transitioning from class to class, to your locker, home to do homework, and then back to school. It's no wonder that keeping track of assignments is so difficult!

Do any of these scenarios sound familiar to you?

☐ "I know I did my homework, but I can't find it now!"

☐ "Oh, no...I brought my science notebook home instead of my math notebook!"

☐ "My bag is so heavy, sometimes I think my back will break!"

☐ "My spiral notebooks get caught on everything: the bottom of my bag, my clothes, each other; they are very annoying."

☐ "I get so many papers and don't have any time to put them away, so they all fall to the bottom of my bag and get crushed."

If you can relate to any of these comments, you are not alone!

Students simply have too much "stuff." Typically, students will have one folder and one notebook for each of their classes; that can be up to 8 folders and 8 notebooks...16 items total! No wonder papers end up all over the place! Wouldn't it be nice if you could condense all of your papers, folders, and notebooks down to one easy-to-manage binder? You can!

The SOAR® Binder System

The SOAR® Binder System solves all of the most common organization problems. It is a very simple and easy way to keep schoolwork organized. It consists of one 1-inch binder that houses folders and notebooks for *all* of your classes.

You are probably wondering:

**"How can I keep seven inches of notebooks and folders
in a one-inch binder? It'll never work!"**

It may seem unlikely, but it is possible. This system has made a significant difference for thousands of students, from grade school to grad school!

Turn This...   Into This!

I can't believe how much easier it is for me to keep my papers organized. Since I started using the SOAR® Binder, I have not lost one assignment! My parents are so excited, and I feel so much better about school. Thank you!

- Michael Zabik, 9th grade student

"How Does It Work?"

In the SOAR® Binder, you replace traditional folders and notebooks with plastic pocket folders and loose-leaf notebook paper. Each plastic folder holds papers for individual classes. It also acts as a divider for notes, which are placed behind the folder. At the end of each marking period, the folders are emptied into a simple "home paper station" to keep the binder from getting overloaded.

The binder travels with you to each class and goes home with you at the end of each day. You never have to worry about taking the wrong folder/notebook to class, or home for homework, because you only have to keep track of one item.

> The SOAR® Binder System is a perfect organizing solution when you live in two homes. You never have to worry about leaving a folder or notebook at the "other" house because everything is in one binder, making it easier to keep papers and notes with you at all times.

"How Do I Create a SOAR® Binder?"

Simply get the supplies listed in Step 1 on the next page, and follow the directions for assembling and using the binder. You can begin using this tomorrow. You will instantly be organized...and easily *stay* organized.

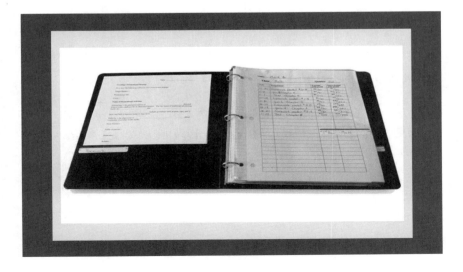

step 1

Gather Materials

- One, 1" diameter binder with pockets on the inside covers*
- One plastic folder for each individual class (Avery Binder Pockets work well.)
- One file folder for each individual class
- Labels for each folder and binder pocket
- Loose-leaf notebook paper

* Stick to a 1" binder. Anything larger is too bulky to carry, so it won't be used. However, if you are *not* allowed to carry a bag in school, you can use a 1½" binder and add a zipper case to hold pens, pencils, and other supplies.

step 2

Put the Pieces Together

- **Place the plastic folders in the binder rings.** The plastic folders work better than traditional folders because they are more durable. They also minimize bulk because you typically will only need one pocket for each class.

- **Place 20-30 sheets of notebook paper behind the last folder at the back of the binder.** As you need to take notes, you will use these notebook papers to write your notes. You can then place your notes behind the folder for that class.

step 3

Label Folders in the Binder

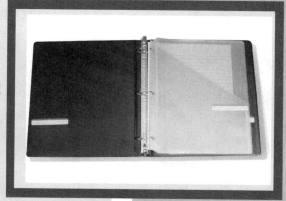

- **Label your folders.** It is very important to label one folder for each class so you do not accidently put papers in the wrong place. A simple label can save a lot of frustration when you are rushed and need to find something in your binder quickly.

- **Label the front pocket of the binder "Homework" and the back pocket of the binder "Miscellaneous."**

Create a Home "Paper Station"

- **Label one file folder for each of your classes and store the file folders in a safe place at home.** A "safe place" may be a small file crate, a shoe box under your bed, a specific drawer in your desk, or even in your parents' filing cabinet. The important thing is to determine one specific place so you will not lose them!

- **Store binder overflow in these file folders.** Periodically (about 1 or 2 times per quarter), remove papers from your binder and put them in the file folders. Do not throw away any papers until after you have received your final grade for each class; these papers will help you create a good study guide for big unit tests or final exams and will also help you prove your grade if a mistake shows up on your report card.

"How Do I Use the SOAR® Binder System?"

The magic of the SOAR® Binder System is in how you use it! Follow the tips below:

Using the Binder in School

NEVER put loose papers inside your book bag! Instead of cramming papers into your bag, just slide them into the front of your binder. Later, when you have a few seconds, you can put the papers in their correct folders.

Don't trash your book bag! When you are in a hurry, simply slide papers under the front cover of your binder instead of stashing them loosely in your bag.

Keep your binder easily accessible throughout the day. Like your planner, keep it on your desk or on top of all of your belongings under the desk. If you have to dig through several things to access it, you won't use it.

Put *all* papers that need your attention at home in the front pocket of the binder. This includes homework papers, notes for your parents, forms that need to be signed, items you want to leave at home, etc. This will save you time at home because you will not have to rifle through several folders to find your homework pages.

Use the back pocket of the binder for "miscellaneous" items. Sometimes you have to hold papers that are not for a specific class, so they may not have a specific folder. Items such as school fundraiser information or a health form for P.E. can be placed in the back pocket of your binder for safe keeping.

Using the Binder at Home

Take two. Take two minutes each evening to put stray papers into the correct folders. It will save a lot of time searching for homework later. If you were rushed in school and had to stash a few papers in the front of your binder, take a few seconds to put them away when you sit down to do your homework. A few seconds each night will save you a lot of time and frustration later.

As you finish homework, immediately put assignments away in the correct folders. Do not wait until you finish *all* of your homework before you put your papers away; this increases the chances of papers getting mixed with other items in your home, put in the wrong folder, or simply forgotten.

Clean out your binder 1 or 2 times per quarter; put the "old" papers in your file folders. It cannot be emphasized enough: do not throw any papers away until you get your report card! Your old papers are a gem for making study guides and will provide evidence if you discover an error in your grades.

Common Questions About Using the SOAR® Binder System

Q: "My teacher requires a separate folder/binder for her class. I don't think I can use the SOAR® Binder System."

A: Most teachers request specific materials to be sure that students have *some* method for organizing supplies for their class. Show your teacher your binder and ask if you can use it. In almost 20 years of teaching this method, I know of only one teacher who insisted on a separate binder for her class. If this happens to you, follow your teacher's wishes. But, continue to use the **SOAR®** Binder System for all of your other classes.

Q: "What if I can't get all of my papers to fit into a 1-inch binder?"

A: Remember to clean out your folders and notes at least once per quarter (possibly twice). Also, make sure you are only using loose-leaf notebook paper and *not* storing spiral notebooks in your binder. If you follow these guidelines, you should have no trouble fitting everything you need into one binder.

Q: "My teacher often collects our notebooks. He will want me to have a spiral notebook...what do I do?"

A: Ask your teacher if you can simply staple your notebook pages together and turn in the packet of papers when he collects notebooks. As mentioned earlier, teachers are usually quite receptive to helping students get and stay organized, so you are not likely to have a problem.

chapter 6

Organize Your Papers

Organize Your Space

Organize Your Time

Cluttered Spaces = Cluttered Minds

Your bedroom, book bag, and locker play a big role in your efficiency in school. Now that your folders and notebooks are in order, it's time to put your space in order, too. Messy spaces can be overwhelming and distracting, not to mention the perfect place to lose homework and other important things.

This chapter will help you create a specific place for all of your things. When things have a "home" space it is easier to keep organized. The chapter is not about being perfectly clean. Its about being able to find what you need, when you need it.

Lessons from the Silverware Sorter

What can a silverware sorter teach us about organization? Basically, everything we need to know!

Here's the scoop…

You can walk into any home in America, whether that be a house, an apartment, a mansion, or a trailer – even a pop-up camper – and you can figure out where the silverware goes.

It could be the messiest home (or camper) in the world, but you *will* find the silverware, thanks to the silverware sorter.

This simple little tool illustrates the two most critical principles of organization:

    1. Items must have a specific, designated place to "live," and

    2. That location must be easy to access.

As you read the rest of this chapter, remember the silverware sorter.

Organize Mission Control: Your Room

Your room is your personal Mission Control, the central space from which you organize your life. A cluttered and chaotic room can have a dramatic effect on your life in school. When your room is organized, you are more likely to keep track of your assignments, do homework, get ready for school, and do just about anything else more efficiently.

Most significantly, you will have a greater feeling of control in your life. It may take a little while to get your room cleaned and organized. However, the following steps will make it easy to *keep* your room organized.

step 1

Remove the Stuff You Don't Need

"Decluttering" is not easy, but it is vital for getting organized. In our disposable society, we accumulate items so fast that our possessions easily overtake our lives. How can you get rid of extra things you don't need?

Label four large boxes (or garbage bags): "Trash," "Donations," "Storage," and "Somewhere Else."

Just as the labels suggest:

 The **Trash Box** is for garbage.

 The **Donations Box** is for used clothes, toys, electronics, and more that are in good condition and can be donated to charity. (This is a great way to help others and recycle at the same time.)

 The **Storage Box** is for items you want to keep but do not need to store in your room. (Ask for your parents' permission before you store your belongings outside of your room.)

 The **Somewhere Else Box** is for items that belong somewhere else in your home. Deliver all items to their correct place all at one time, later.

Storage Tip

If you must put items in "storage," clearly label the outside of all containers.

One way to keep storage items under control is to limit yourself to one large box, especially for keepsakes. If an item does not fit in your box, then it is time to get rid of something.

Group Similar Items Together

Begin sorting items by category.

Some examples include:

- ❑ Electronic equipment
- ❑ Stuffed animals
- ❑ Trophies and awards
- ❑ Notes and pictures of friends
- ❑ Sports equipment
- ❑ Music equipment (instruments, etc.)
- ❑ School supplies and your Home "Paper Station"
- ❑ Books
- ❑ Computer and computer supplies
- ❑ Clothes (Are they overstuffed in drawers or closets?)
- ❑ Supplies/materials for a special hobby
- ❑ "Not sure" pile (for things that don't seem to belong with anything else.)
- ❑ _____
- ❑ _____
- ❑ _____

Find a Place for Everything

Create a specific place for everything. This is the key step to *keeping* your room organized. Consider the following storage suggestions:

Space under the bed is good for storing items such as shoes and bedding. Put items in containers that will slide out easily so you can get everything easily. There are several storage containers on the market for use under standard beds. The top lids of boxes also work nicely.

Use the top of tall bookcases and dressers. These are good places to store things that you do not need to access regularly, such as stuffed animals and trophies.

Look up! Many closets have a lot of unused space above the top shelf. Consider storing large items such as luggage and sleeping bags in these spaces. (Would the sleeping bag fit inside the luggage?)

A large bulletin board is a great place to post pictures, notes from friends, special keepsakes, ribbons, and other 2-dimensional items. In addition to keeping desk and dresser tops free of clutter, they can add a nice dimension to your room. You can dress up a standard bulletin board with fabric (like the one pictured to the left) or by spray painting it to match your room.

Trunks provide great storage and added seating space for visiting friends. However, trunk space should not be used to store small items that will easily get lost in the deep space. Consider using trunks for storing extra bedding, bulky sweaters, sports/music equipment, or other large items.

Plastic crates are ideal for items such as books, school supplies, electronics, and small sports equipment. Crates are ideal storage pieces because their utility is flexible; their use can change as your needs and interests change. Secondly, the stackable nature of the crates makes good use of vertical storage, which is commonly unused space.

Organize Your Study Space

Where do you do your homework? In your bedroom? In the kitchen? Near the computer? Someplace else? No matter where you do your homework, it is important that you have a place with few distractions so you can do your homework quickly.

Maximize your study space with the following tips:

Keep a bucket or basket supplied with pens, pencils, eraser, stapler, tape, paper, and markers. This container can easily move with you if you need to do homework in different rooms.

Make your space comfortable. Snazz it up with a poster, flowers, holiday lights…. Making your study space more inviting will help to make the process of doing homework a bit more enjoyable.

Keep lighting and temperature at comfortable levels. The lighting should be comfortable for you...not too dim, but not too bright. Likewise, the room temperature should not be extreme. Lighting and temperature play a big role in helping you stay focused.

Use music that promotes concentration. You can find many sources of music that specifically promote concentration, in app stores and online music stores. (Search "music for concentration.") The sound-waves generated by this type of music match the frequencies as brainwaves in a state of learning and high concentration. This type of music helps your brain focus very quickly and minimizes distractions. If you live in an active house, it will help you mask background noise. It also works well *as* background noise if you can't concentrate when it is "too quiet."

Organize Your Locker

freesoulproduction/Shutterstock

Keep trash out of your locker! When you are in a rush for class, you can't afford to be rifling through a lot of junk trying to find your books.

Store morning books flat and afternoon books standing upright. This tactic helps you find books quickly for two reasons. One, they are neatly organized. Secondly, it is easier to pull textbooks out of two smaller, lighter piles than one tall, heavy pile. If you have covers on your textbooks, label the spines clearly so you don't grab the wrong book.

As you visit your locker throughout the day, place books needed for homework on the floor of your locker. (Just be sure you don't have water or melting snow on your coat that will drip onto your books.)

Keep morning books flat and
afternoon books standing upright.

Organize Your Book Bag

The greatest weapon against a messy book bag is the SOAR® Binder! The primary cause of a disorganized bag is the collection of loose papers that collect in the bottom, getting crushed and crumpled by the rest of your books.

Always use your binder to keep papers in order; this cannot be emphasized enough! If you are in a rush and don't have time to put papers in their proper folders, just slide them inside the front of your binder and organize them later. This simple step will save many hours of searching for papers lost in the depths of your book bag. And it will prevent you from losing points on lost homework that you know you did!

Before you head home at the end of the school day, take one last look in your locker. Check to make sure you haven't left behind books or supplies that you will need for homework.

design56/Shutterstock

Check your bag before you go to bed at night. Make sure you have everything you need for school the next day, *especially* your binder.

Conclusion

This chapter provides strategies for keeping your belongings organized. You do not have to be a "neat freak" to stay organized. You should simply identify places for your belongings and try to keep them in place. Like everything else, it will be easier for some people than others, but is a great habit to develop.

> It is a wonderful feeling when you have control over your clutter, instead of your clutter having control over you!

Learning how to organize your things will benefit you for the rest of your life, saving time and allowing you to be more productive. It is a wonderful feeling when you have control over your clutter, instead of your clutter having control over you!

Now that your space is organized, you will notice many parts of your life getting easier, having less friction. The next chapter will take you one step further on the path to efficiency....

chapter 7

Organize Your Papers
Organize Your Space

Organize Your Time

To make time for your fun, "pebble" priorities, it is important to organize your time. Of course, you have to be flexible to handle unexpected events. However, there are several ways to use your time more efficiently. The process of "organizing your time" automatically happens as you follow some of the strategies already described in this book. Some sections of this chapter are a review, but they are revisited in this chapter in the full context of organizing your time.

Develop Routines

Routines are a powerful way to organize your time, for things you do regularly. The more "automatic" these tasks are for you, the easier they will be and the less time they will take.

Research suggests that a person has to do something 7 to 21 times before it becomes a habit. So developing routines can take time, but the time you save in the long run is worth it. There are a few specific routines that can especially maximize your time:

Use a planner every day! Record all of the things you need to do at home *or* in school. Don't forget to write down test dates, project due dates, books you need to take home, and permission slips that need to be signed. Make it a point to look at it when you get home and double-check it before you go to bed.

Initiate "Sunday Night Meetings" with your parents. As mentioned on page 51, tell your parents about your sports practices/games, due dates, supplies you may need for a special project, etc. Be sure to ask them what their schedules look like for the week. (They'll be impressed with your consideration of their schedule.) If your parents are separated, be sure you talk to both of them about the upcoming week.

Avoid rushed and chaotic mornings. Mornings are hectic for most people. The most common homework excuse I heard from my students was "Things were so busy this morning, I forgot my homework on the kitchen table." The solution is simple: prepare the night before.

7-21
...is the number of attempts required to develop a habit.

Before you go to bed on a school night, you should:

- ❑ Put all of your papers in your binder and make sure they are in the correct folder.

- ❑ Double-check your planner to make sure you took care of everything that needed your attention: homework, notes that need to be signed, field trip money, etc.

- ❑ Gather your binder, planner, all of your books, lunch money, and other necessary supplies and place them in your bag. Don't forget about any gear you may need for things such as dance class or track practice.

- ❑ Put your bag by the door you will exit in the morning.

- ❑ Pick out your clothes for the next day to save the time of deliberating over what to wear and to prevent a last-minute search for your favorite pair of jeans or shoes.

Maximize Your Time

Have you ever noticed how much time is "wasted" in a school day? There are several ways you can maximize this otherwise unused time:

Take advantage of "down time" in school. Some studies say that only 50-60% of a student's school day is actually spent on productive lessons or related activities. The rest of the time is spent: taking attendance, waiting for other students, school announcements, classroom interruptions, etc. Take advantage of that "down time!" Open your binder and review your notes from a few previous classes, pull out your math assignment and do a few problems, read the next section of your science textbook, etc. Many students complete most, if not all, of their homework in school by using this down time to their advantage.

Take advantage of "down time" during after-school activities. Just as you can find windows of time during school, you can often find small chunks of time while waiting for activities after school.

Do you have a long bus ride? Even if you spend 15 minutes working on some homework or reviewing your notes, it's 15 more minutes you'll have for yourself at home. Of course, sometimes it is nice to socialize with friends on the bus ride to and from school, which is okay; it will help you relax a bit after school and get refreshed before starting homework.

Make your week even more efficient... gathering your clothes once per week is a lot more efficient than doing it every day.

Do your homework as early in the afternoon as possible. While it is important to give yourself a little break after school, the break should be no more than 45 minutes. The sooner you can start homework, the sooner it will be done. If you wait until later in the evening, you won't be quite as fresh, and the work will take longer.

Power down! Turn off your cell phone, TV, radio, and computer. No matter who you are, there is always a temptation to do two things at once. But it is impossible for you to concentrate on more than one thing at a time (your brain is not capable of processing more than one set of audio or visual input at one time.) "Multi-tasking" is really just a process of your brain's attention playing rapid-fire ping-pong, back-and-forth between tasks or between TV and homework, etc. Do yourself the favor of getting your homework done and out of the way, then you can enjoy your electronics without the stress of homework to bog you down!

Conclusion

No one is ever perfect at managing time, but this chapter covers ways you can optimize your time.

Now that you have established your goals and organized all parts of your life, it is time to learn some easy and effective study strategies in the next section, *Ask questions.*

Time-Management Challenge

The hours between 3 & 6 p.m. are typically the most poorly used hours of the day.

Are there some ways you can make those hours more productive for yourself?

Organize
-Summary-

1   **Organizing skills are learned.** They are not skills that some people are born with and others without. Learning how to organize will help you gain confidence and a greater sense of control in your life, making success easier to achieve.

2   **The SOAR® Binder System is a simple solution for keeping notes, assignments, and all school-related materials in one convenient location.** Among many benefits: it prevents homework from getting lost, keeps your book bag clean, and reduces the weight you have to carry around by eliminating spiral notebooks.

3   **Clutter creates a distracting environment.** Keeping your space organized will help you be much more efficient and successful in school. The key to keeping clutter under control is to create a specific place for each of your belongings.

4   **Create more time for "fun stuff" in your life.** Developing routines and making use of otherwise wasted time will allow you to have more time for your "water" and "pebble" priorities.

Ask questions

section 4

Ask questions

Check all statements below that apply to you:

_____ Sometimes I have a hard time communicating effectively.

_____ I sometimes do not know what questions to ask in class.

_____ I have a hard time remembering information when I read a textbook.

_____ I think I could do a better job of taking notes and using my notes to study for tests.

_____ I don't take tests very well. I think I know the information, but I'm often disappointed with my scores.

_____ When I have to write a paper, I don't even know where to start.

_____ I get nervous when I have to give an oral presentation.

_____ I can't remember all the rules of language for spelling, grammar, and punctuation.

You will find solutions to these problems, and much more, in the following section.

> Knowledge is having the right answer.
>
> Intelligence is asking the right question.

How does "asking questions" help you get better grades in less time?
The best way to understand the power of questions is to learn how your brain works.

How Your Brain Works

Your brain is made of billions of tiny wires, called neurons. Every time you learn something new, your brain grows new neuron wires. That means every time you learn something new, you change the structure of your brain! But those neuron wires can only grow if they are connected to wires that already exist. New brain wires must literally "plug in" to existing brain wires for power.

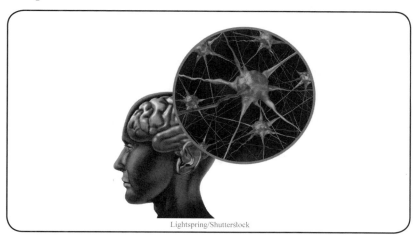

Lightspring/Shutterstock

In other words, the *only* way to learn something new is to "attach" the new information to something you already understand!
Read that again. This is the foundation of learning; connecting new information to old information.

People sometimes argue claiming that "connections" are *not* required for learning. They claim that they have studied for tests – and often done well on them –but didn't really understand anything they studied.

Can you relate to that situation? I certainly can because I did this for years…before I learned *how* to learn. I now understand that I was not actually learning…I was memorizing.

When you memorize information, you simply spin it through your short-term memory, which is an actual section of your brain. But, as its name suggests, short-term memory can only hold information for a short time. It has a very limited capacity and consumes a lot of brain energy. The moment it can let go of information, it will.

Growing "Growth Mindsets" & Grit

In her landmark book, *Mindset,* Carol Dweck, Ph.D., shares her scientific research on motivation. She concluded that teaching students how to learn, in conjunction with brain biology, is the best way to boost motivation and develop a "growth mindset." In two scientific studies, she confirmed that this combination works; motivation and grades skyrocketed among adolescents! Angela Duckworth, Ph.D., cites Dweck's work as one of the strongest ways for students to develop "grit"…the character trait most strongly associated with success!

This is why many people turn in a test, then feel like they immediately forgot everything they memorized. They did! The information was never learned in the first place.

The only way information will stick long-term is if new information is connected to something you already understand. Information that you already know is stored in the areas of the brain that manage long-term storage and recall.

When you connect new information to previously mastered information, you automatically drag it out of short-term memory and fuse it into your long-term memory. You might get a better sense of this by thinking about a time when your neurons did *not* connect.

Have you ever asked a question and received an answer you didn't understand? We often describe that situation by saying the answer went "over our head." Now, replay that experience in very slow motion. The exact moment that you heard the answer, you were expecting to understand it. Then suddenly, you realized you didn't. For that brief moment in between, there was great confusion. It was so unexpected, you may have slightly shaken your head or adjusted your physical position, feeling like you briefly lost you balance. Guess what? You did!

"Low-gear" learning is like taking the long, scenic route.

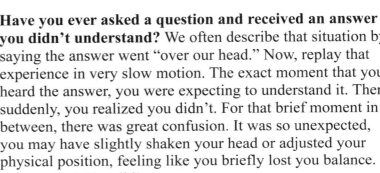

spirit of americaShutterstock

Well, actually, the neurons in your brain lost their balance. When you asked the question, your brain set up neurons, ready to connect to an answer. But, the answer did not make sense to you. So, those neurons were not able to grab the new information; they were left without a connection. You *felt* "off balance" because your neurons were literally unbalanced.

Again, the important lesson here is that learning only happens when you connect new information to something you already understand. This is why questions are so valuable…they naturally create these valuable connections in your brain.

Low-Gear vs High-Gear Learning

I live in Detroit. If I want to drive to Chicago, which is 300 miles away, I have two routes I can take: the interstate freeway or an old county road. On the county road, the speed limit never goes above 55 mph. In fact, it drops to 25 mph when passing through many of the small towns along the way. The country road also has many: intersections, stop lights, and stop signs. On the other hand, the interstate freeway has no stops and the speed limit is mostly 70 mph.

Which route should I take? By most measures, the interstate freeway is the best option. I will get there faster. It will require less fuel. And it will cause less wear and tear on the brakes and engine of my car. The only reason to take the old county road is if I want to enjoy the scenery (and I have extra time).

When it comes to schoolwork, no one wants the long, scenic route. People want to get their work and studying done as quickly as possible. They want the "interstate freeway" option.

I call this "high-gear" learning. Like the interstate, high-gear learning is the faster option. It uses less brain power. It is less wear and tear on your energy, attitude, and emotions. In fact, when you shift into "high-gear" learning, you will actually *feel* more energetic!

However, when it comes to learning, most people operate in "low gear." Memorizing is a great example of low-gear learning; it is completely inefficient and ineffective. It's like taking the long, slow, scenic route with lots of stops and interruptions along the way.

Alex Ionas/Shutterstock

"High-gear" learning is the faster way to learn, *and* it is more effective.

So, how do you shift into high-gear learning? You ask questions.

Why? Because questions naturally connect to long-term memory. Your long-term memory is far more powerful and deeply connected; it is specifically built for long-term understanding and recall.

If you can create questions, you can master:

- working with others,
- reading textbooks,
- taking notes,
- studying for tests,
- writing research papers,
- giving speeches,
- and a whole lot more!

The chapters that follow show you how this simple little concept – creating questions to build connections –can be extraordinarily powerful!

Look for the 80/20 Power Strategies!
(See page 21)

Every chapter in this section has one.

chapter 8
How to Speak
& Listen Effectively

speaking • listening • reading comprehension • writing

"What Makes People Successful in the Workplace?"

Researchers interviewed hundreds of CEOs, from the world's largest companies, to answer this question. Their conclusion? It's not what people "know" that was most important.

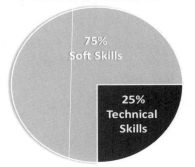

Career Success Is:

75% Soft Skills

25% Technical Skills

Communication skills are ranked FIRST among a job candidate's "must have" skills and qualities, according to the National Association of Colleges and Employers.

– 2010 Survey, NACE

The path to success is determined by people's ability to work with others and manage themselves. They concluded 75% of long-term career success depends on "soft skills." (In education, we call them "study skills" or "learning skills.") Only 25% of career success depends on technical knowledge. In other words, all of your years in school only contribute to *one-fourth* of the equation for career success.

The ability to work effectively with others and manage yourself is 75% of your success equation! We've already covered several chapters about "managing yourself" in school: setting goals, managing your time, and getting organized.

Now it's time to learn how to work effectively with other people. In the workplace, you will have to work with co-workers, vendors, a boss, and often your boss's boss. You will likely have customers or clients to serve, as well. The ability to work with others is vital! The key to effectively working with others is to have solid communication skills.

"Why Are Communication Skills Important in School?"

Working with teachers can have a dramatic impact on your grades! (You'll discover why in the next chapter.) Group work is often assigned in school. And, let's face it… school is much more fun when you enjoy the people around you!

There is one skill that will catapult your communication skills! It's an 80/20 Power Strategy for becoming a top-quality communicator; it is the ability to ask questions.

"How Do Questions Improve Communication?"

All communication rests on knowing the answer to one question…

marekuliasz/Shutterstock

Why are you speaking?

Why did the author write what you are reading?

Why is your friend telling you something?

Why do you want to write that email to your teacher?

This simple question clarifies the purpose of the communication.
It clarifies your purpose when you express yourself. It also helps you
understand speakers or authors when they are expressing themselves.

**Knowing the purpose for communicating provides vital clarity in
creating or receiving messages.** If you don't understand the purpose for
writing a specific report, you will have a very hard time writing that report,
and you will most likely include a lot of useless information.

If you don't understand your teacher's purpose for giving a lecture,
you will have a very hard time understanding the lecture. Pretty soon,
you'll be totally spaced-out and daydreaming.

If you don't understand why your friend is telling you a story, you will
likely miss out on the feelings – or other important messages – he or she is
trying to share.

The "purpose" for every communication becomes the "thing" to which
you connect all of the other details.

Follow the Models for Clear Communication

**The communication models on pages 88 and 89 appear frequently
throughout this section.** They illustrate how everything you express or
understand starts with the key question, "Why?" Then the model shows
you how to use the *purpose* of the communication to improve your
speaking, writing, listening, and reading comprehension.

Communication Model for Speaking & Writing

Expressive Communication: conversing ● presenting ● writing papers ● composing emails

We all have the desire to express ourselves, but have you ever felt tongue-tied in the middle of a conversation? Have you ever had writer's block trying to write a paper? If so, you probably were not clear on your purpose. The model below will help you identify your purpose for speaking or writing. Then, you will use your purpose to figure out exactly what to say or write.

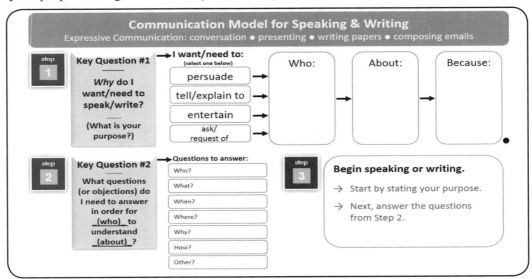

How to Use This Model

Create Your Purpose Statement

For example if you need to write an email to your teacher asking for help, the more clarity you have about your question, the faster you will write and the better your teacher will understand your needs. If you follow the prompts from the model, you'll create a purpose sentence like this:

I want to <u>ask</u> <u>my teacher</u> <u>about getting additional help</u> <u>because I have been</u>
  (expression type)   (who)   (about)   (because)
<u>confused about the last two homework assignments.</u>

List Potential Questions the Other Person May Have

In this case, think about the questions your teacher may have about what you need. (Listed in this step you will find the most common question starters. But, you can create more.) Some questions your teacher may ask include:

> What problems are causing you trouble?
> Where are you getting stuck?
> What have you tried to do?

Begin Writing or Speaking

For example, begin writing the email to your teacher by first stating your reason (purpose) for writing. Then write answers to the questions you developed in Step 2.

Communication Model for Listening & Comprehension

Receptive Communication: conversation ● lectures ● videos ● reading

Have you ever "zoned out" during a lecture, conversation, or while reading? Your brain "zones out" when it cannot make connections to what it is hearing or reading. To make meaningful connections, you must know the *speaker* or *author's* purpose. Not knowing the purpose is like trying to build a house without a floor; there's nothing to which the walls can attach!

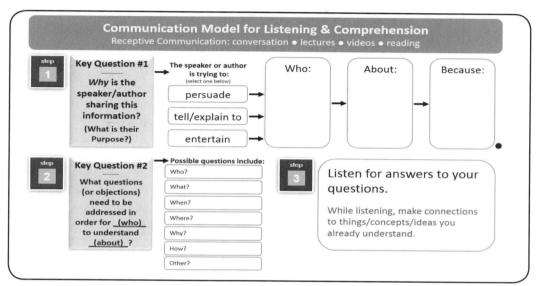

How to Use This Model

This model is nearly identical to the Speaking & Writing model on the previous page. The only difference is your perspective!

step 1

Identify the Speaker or Author's Purpose by Completing the Sentence-Builder from their Perspective.

For example, if you are listening to a lecture about the periodic table, your sentence might look like this:

The speaker (my teacher) <u>is trying to explain</u> <u>to students</u> <u>about the different parts</u>
                                    (expression type)   (who)   (about)
<u>of the periodic table</u> <u>because the entire chemistry class is based on this chart.</u>
                                            (because)

IMPORTANT: If you have trouble determining the speaker or author's purpose, don't stress! It simply means you need further clarification from your teacher. The important thing is that you have *identified* your confusion clearly and quickly. See page 93 for more information.

step 2

List Potential Questions That Need to be Addressed

What questions will the speaker or author need to answer in order to accomplish their "purpose?"

step 3

Listen for Answers to Your Questions

While listening for answers, make connections to things, concepts, or ideas with which you are familiar.

chapter 9

How to Work with Teachers & Peers

How to Work with Teachers

Why is it important to work with teachers? Complete the activity below for a visual explanation.

Directions: Draw the floor plan (bird's eye view) of one of your classrooms in the box below. Use the key to represent the appropriate people and furniture in the room.

Key

☒ = student desk

☑ = teacher desk

↑ = door (entrance to room)

▯ = classroom closet and/or cabinets

◼ = table

▭ = file cabinet

☺ = you

✪ = your teacher

"How Can This Map Help Me Work with Teachers?"

If your map is close to scale, you will see that you represent one small part of a much larger classroom. Consider this from a teacher's perspective…. Your teachers are required to teach and supervise a lot of students each day. Usually, teachers have 20-36 students per class, up to 150 students per day. To most effectively help you, your teachers *first* need your help.

Ask Questions!

You need to stand out from the crowd… in a positive way. One teacher cannot possibly give proper attention to more than 100 students every day, so raise your hand to ask a reasonable question once in a while (beyond asking if you can go the restroom). Or contribute to class discussions. If you're not comfortable asking questions in front of others, stay after class. The chapters that follow provide additional tips to help you identify good questions to ask in class; simply look for the "Teacher Talking Point" icon, as pictured on the right margin.

"How Can I Raise My Grades by Asking Questions?"

Teachers usually have some flexibility with assigning grades. If teachers see that you care about your work, this can work to your favor. For example, they may be willing to give half-credit on an incorrect math problem or overlook a few spelling errors on an essay because they know you put in effort. At the end of a term, they may add one or two points to give you a boost into a higher letter grade.

When applying for college, scholarships, and jobs, you will need letters of recommendation from teachers. A powerful letter from a teacher will often be a deciding factor over other candidates.

In addition, teachers are often great leads for internships and jobs. Teachers are often asked by business owners to recommend "responsible and reliable" students for hire. Employers like to have recommendations from teachers who can hand-pick their best students, those who have stood out as responsible and respectful.

Need to Write an Email to Your Teacher?

See "How to Write an Email" at: www.StudySkills.com/bonus-edu.

"Afraid to Ask a Question in Class?"

Perhaps you tuned out for a while and think the teacher may have just answered your question?

This happens to everyone, even adults. When you are in this situation, simply raise your hand and say, "You may have already answered this, but I missed it. Can you please explain…?" Most teachers will appreciate your respectfulness and will be happy to answer your question.

How to Be a Great Listener in Class

In the previous chapter, the Listening and Comprehension Model was introduced. It simplifies effective listening down to three basic steps:

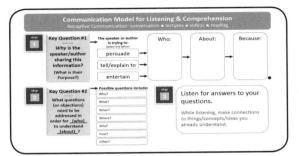

 step 1 Identify the speaker's purpose.

 step 2 **Brainstorm a list of questions** the speaker might need to answer to accomplish his/her purpose.

step 3 Listen for answers to the questions.

The next time you doze off during a lecture or "zone out" when your teacher is talking, don't worry about remembering *all* of these steps. To rein in your brain, simply remember three key words…

Listen for Answers!

Play Jeopardy™, quietly in your head, by imagining questions for the topics your teacher is explaining. This process of flipping information into questions engages your attention. It will force you to think about connections you can make to the content. It forces you to think about the purpose of the lecture.

Yes, your mind will be buzzing! But now it will be focused on what your teacher is saying. For example, if your teacher is lecturing about how to be a great listener in class, you can ask yourself:

> *"What questions could she be answering?*
>
> *"Well, first, I have to figure out her purpose for this lecture. So why is she telling us this information? Let's see, she's explaining to us about how to be a great listener because we have to do a lot of listening in class…and it's boring.*

"Now, what kinds of questions could she be answering? Here are a few: Is it really possible for listening to not be boring? How can listening get easier? What can we actually do? Who does this well? When should we be listening? Why does it work? Why should I care?"

The dialogue in your head may be slightly distracting, but you'll miss much more information if you don't attempt to craft questions. This process gives your brain a purpose for "catching" information. You can literally train your own brain to be more attentive.

What If You Don't Know Your Teacher's "Purpose?"

The speaker's purpose is the "hook" that lets you make all of the valuable connections for learning. It is essential to understand the "purpose" behind any information you are trying to understand!

But what if you can't figure out the main purpose for today's lecture? Don't fret! This situation is common; most students sit in class, simply "going through the motions," without ever being engaged. The moment you make a commitment to follow a lecture, you're already several steps ahead!

If you can't figure out the purpose, you've simply done yourself the great favor of quickly determining that you need some clarification. So now you have two choices:

1. **Raise your hand and ask!** As you just learned, there are many benefits to asking questions in class. For example, you can say: "Can you please describe the main purpose of today's lecture? If you already covered it, I'm sorry, but I missed it." Simple enough. But if you're not comfortable with this option, go with the next option….

Scott Maxwell/LuMaxArtShutterstock

2. **Make a guess.** It is far better to make a guess about your teacher's purpose than to remain unengaged. So make your best guess…then listen for answers and connections. (However, it is still a good idea to ask your teacher for clarification after class.)

Listen for Connections

In addition to "listening for answers," listen for connections. Can you relate what the teacher is describing to something else? Can you draw a visual image or diagram of what he's saying?

Make a connection to anything! If your teacher mentions that the Declaration of Independence was signed in Philadelphia, and it makes you think of cream cheese, that's great! Just picture John Hancock signing his name nice and big with a feather pen in one hand and a big bagel with cream cheese in the other. These connections may seem zany, but they will make the neurons in your brain go giddy with excitement because…they are making connections!

More Tips for Paying Attention in Class

Listening for answers and connections is the most powerful thing you can do to pay attention in class! But if you're feeling drowsy or find yourself daydreaming, there's more you can do:

❑ **Start with good sleep and a healthy breakfast.** Sleep and food are essential for concentration.

❑ **Stretch your eye muscles.** Tired eyes can make the rest of your body feel fatigued, too. To stretch your eye muscles:

l i g h t p o e t/Shutterstock

1. Close your eyes. Gently massage your eyes, over your eyelids for 10-20 seconds.

2. Keep your eyes closed. Roll your eyeballs up towards the inside of your head. Hold them in place for 10 seconds.

3. Continue to close your eyes. Roll your eyeballs down as if you were trying to see your teeth. Hold for another 10 seconds.

4. Finally, keep your lids closed. Roll your eyes up so they are facing directly in front of you. Open your eyes. Repeat as needed.

Improve your circulation. Your body's circulation slows down after sitting for 30-40 minutes. This is usually when people begin to feel restless or drowsy in class. Some ways to rev up your circulation include:

❑ **Move.** Get your blood pumping to reenergize quickly. If it is possible, get up and walk around for a few minutes. Do jumping jacks in the restroom if you have to.

❑ **Adjust your posture.** If you are not able to get out of your seat, improve your posture. After sitting for a while, your shoulders slump over. You cross your legs. You slouch in your chair. All of these positions restrict your circulation. So, sit up straight. Uncross your legs. Lean slightly forward. Smile! You'll feel refreshed right away!

❑ **Breathe deep.** Normal breathing only circulates the top third of the oxygen in our lungs. Deep breathing replaces the bottom two-thirds with fresh, revitalizing oxygen. An effective way to breathe deeply is:

1. Adjust your posture (as described above).

2. Inhale as deep and slow as you can.

3. Hold your breath as long as you can.

4. Exhale even more slowly than your inhale.

5. Repeat three times to revive the oxygen in your system.

❑ **Stretch your arms and legs. Again, adjust your posture, then** S-T-R-E-E-E-E-E-T-C-H your arms and legs as much as you can without disrupting class

How to Work with Peers

"If there is any one secret of success, it lies in the ability to get the other person's point of view and see things from that angle, as well as your own."

- Henry Ford

The 80/20 Power Strategy for working with peers is to consider the perspectives of others! People who take the time to consider other people's points of view easily earn respect, friendship, and loyalty. They often avoid conflict because they take time to think about situations from many different perspectives.

Be aware of "non-verbal" messages. When speaking face-to-face, the words you say *only* communicate 7% of your message! According to *Psychology Today* magazine, 55% of your message is expressed with body language and 38% from your tone of voice. If this seems hard to believe, think about how you talk to dogs and babies. It doesn't matter what you say to them…it's all about *how* you say it.

As humans, we never outgrow the impact of non-verbal signals; we simply build additional language skills as we get older. Watch the signals you send with your:

- **Eyes** – Are they focused or wandering? Energetic or tired?

- **Facial gestures** – Are you smiling or looking serious? (HINT: If you're not smiling, you look serious.)

- **Posture** – Is your body upright or slouched? Are you relaxed or tense? Are you leaning in, looking interested, or leaning backwards, looking disengaged?

- **Arms** – Are they relaxed and open or folded and closing others off?

- **Speech** – Are you speaking clearly? Are you using a friendly tone of voice?

How Is Your Message Communicated?

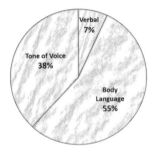

The words we say only communicate 7% of our message! The rest of our message is communicated by tone of voice and body language.

Use active listening. Just as speaking is about more than *saying* words, listening is about more than *hearing* words. You must show you are listening by:

- **Making eye contact.** Look directly at the speaker.

- **Leaning towards the speaker.** Lean in slightly, with a straight spine and relaxed shoulders.

- **Keeping arms relaxed and open.** Do not cross your arms, which closes others out.

- **Asking questions.** When relevant and appropriate, ask for details to show interest.

- **Rephrase what the person said.** Confirm your understanding by restating the message in your own words.

Pay attention to the nonverbal cues used by hosts of talk shows. You will see many of these cues in action! (Hint: Jimmy Fallon is one of the best at using effective – and positive – nonverbal cues!)

How to Collaborate With Groups Effectively

Humans are social beings; we learn most naturally when we can talk, work, and collaborate with others. Yet group collaboration often creates frustration. Students often feel "lost," not sure how to get started or what each person should do. Additional frustration kicks in when group members fail to meet deadlines, making one person or a few other people pick up their slack.

Ilin Sergey/Shutterstock

Your teachers have to determine how to handle the stragglers. (In "the real world," stragglers usually have consequences, such as missing out on a raise or promotion. Or getting fired. Just sayin'.) But I can share tips to optimize the effectiveness of group work:

1. **Know the group's purpose!** A crystal clear purpose will prevent all kinds of problems. Use the Speaking and Writing Model on page 88 to set a clear purpose for the project.

2. **Listen actively and be courteous.** This is a simple reminder to be *intentional* about listening and being friendly. Your efforts will go a long way!

3. **Determine roles for group members –and deadlines!** The process works like this:
   - Break the project into small steps.
   - Arrange steps in chronological order.
   - Set a deadline for each step.
   - Assign the steps to various members of the group.

4. **Determine how you will collaborate.** Meetings? School's online system? Social media platform?

5. **Put all of the information from #3 & #4 in writing and share it with your group.** It is always best to provide information both electronically (via email or online platform) and on paper.

6. **Record all of *your* deadlines in your planner.** Keep the list of group deadlines as a reference, but only add your deadlines to your planner.

7. **Communicate frequently.** Watch deadlines. If you are going to miss a deadline, notify your group as soon as possible, always at least 36 hours in advance.

8. **Beware of "group-think."** It is common for people to agree with ideas simply because other group members appear to agree. Just because other people are nodding does not mean they have thought about the idea. They may not even be listening. If you disagree, speak up! Politely, of course.

9. **Resolve conflicts quickly.** If disagreements are brewing, address them right away. Don't ignore them, hoping things will get better. They never do. See the next section for details on handing conflict effectively.

10. **Celebrate success!** Once the project is done, send a message to thank the other members. It only takes a few seconds and is a great way to build connections with others.

Conflict Resolution: Resolve Disagreements Quickly & Effectively

Almost all conflict happens due to gaps in communication. However, conflict often shrinks – or disappears – as both parties begin to understand each other's point of view. So, once again, the Communication Model for Listening & Comprehension on page 89 is your top resource for mending conflicts.

The Win-Win Outcome

In sports, there is almost always one "winner" and one "loser." In the game of conflict resolution, however, no one should lose if you seek win-win solutions. "Win-win" means both parties are happy…and *everyone* wins. Guidelines for reaching win-win solutions include:

Zorabc/Shutterstock

1. **Cool off.** Don't react; take time to choose your response. When you are upset, you must get away from the situation. Take a nap. Go for a walk. Wait a day. Whatever you do, get space from the problem.

2. **Set the stage.** Agree to work things out calmly. Prepare to use "active listening" posture (see page 96) and a neutral (not angry or agitated) tone of voice.

3. **Start on common ground.** Begin by outlining what both parties agree on.

4. **Identify the problem.** Name exactly what the disagreement or conflict is about. Often, this clarity resolves the problem.

5. **Defuse the problem.** Be sympathetic to the other person. Dale Carnegie, the world's leading authority on people skills for over 100 years, had two "go-to" phrases to express sympathy during conflict:

   1. "I may be wrong, I often am, but let's look at what we know…"

   2. "I don't blame you for feeling the way you do. If I were you, I'd feel the same way."

6. **Brainstorm solutions.** It's time to get creative! Aim for a win-win resolution.

7. **Affirm, forgive, or thank.** It is very important to "close" any type of conflict to be 100% clear that the issue is resolved. Otherwise, the conflict will fester and continue to cause problems. Take a few moments to confirm that the other person is comfortable. If necessary, ask for forgiveness…and thank him or her for working with you.

chapter 10
How to Read Textbooks & Nonfiction

Have you ever read something, only to have no idea *what* you just read? This "brain blackout" is very common when reading about topics that are of little interest to you. And, let's face it, most school reading is *not* at the top of your "high-interest" list.

On the bright side, there are simple ways to dramatically improve comprehension, especially when reading textbooks. To understand why it works, first try the following activity:

What Is It *Really* Like to Read a Textbook?

❶ Turn to page 159 and look at the picture on that page for ONLY 5 seconds. Then move on to step 2.

❷ Now, turn to page 160 and answer as many questions as you can.

❸ Check your answers at the bottom of page 160.

"What's the Point?"

The five questions on page 160 are very simple. But most people struggle just to get one or two answers right. Why the challenge?

The picture is crazy-busy! There are so many things in the photo, you didn't know where to focus your attention. If you had read the questions *first*, they would have been easy to answer because your brain would have known the *purpose* for looking at the photo.

Most students read textbooks in the same way you just looked at the crazy photo…with no *purpose*. Understanding what you read is much easier when you begin with a purpose for reading. Just as the five simple questions about the photo would have been easier to answer if you had known them *before* looking at the photo.

Prime Your Brain for Reading

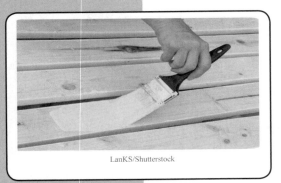

LanKS/Shutterstock

Before you paint a surface for the first time, you have to apply a coat of primer so the paint will stick. Primer is a sticky, paint-like substance that keeps paint from flaking off surfaces. Your brain needs to be primed before you read. Otherwise, new information will "flake" right out of your mind.

New information can only be learned when it is connected to something you already understand. Since you probably don't have many (or any) connections to the content in a textbook, you have to create your own connections. Step 1, below, is the 80/20 Power Strategy for reading textbooks!

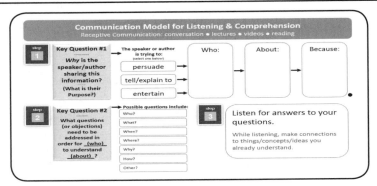

The following three steps correlate with the three steps of the Comprehension Model. Yet they provide a few twists to make the process of reading textbooks even easier!

step 1a **Find the purpose of the text: read the visuals.** I call this process visual networking™; use all visuals in the chapter to make connections. Follow this three-step process:

1. Look at each picture, graph, table, and chart.
2. Read the captions for each visual.
3. Ask yourself, "Why do I think this picture is here?" Don't skip this step; this is where your brain makes connections!

HINT: Connect the visuals to the title of the chapter. Your connection does not have to be accurate: even if it's wrong, you are still building connections! If your connection is not accurate, you will quickly notice the correction when you read the text.

Purpose: Your brain can process visuals much more efficiently than words, which is what makes visual networking™ so powerful! Also, images are expensive for publishers, so they carefully select visuals that best summarize the main idea of the topic.

Find the purpose of the text; read the summary questions.

Purpose: Summary questions provide clear clues about the most important elements of the text. However, these questions are only useful *after* you've "read the visuals," so that you can understand the questions. In fact, you may already be able to answer 30-80% of the questions after reading the

As you read, turn headings into questions.

For example, if the heading is "Volcano Islands," ask, "What are volcano islands?" If the heading is "Exploring Earth's Oceans," you might ask, "Why explore Earth's oceans?" Or, "How do you explore Earth's oceans?"

Purpose: The process of creating questions instantly shifts your brain into high-gear learning. Now your brain is firing neurons that are thirsty to connect with answers!

Read to answer your "heading questions."

Purpose: Your brain *naturally* seeks information *only* to answer questions. So reading to answer your "heading questions" naturally allows your brain to focus on finding an answer. This process quickly improves your reading speed and instantly sharpens your comprehension.

Time-Saving Tip

Save study time by reading your textbook before class. This saves time because:

- You will get far more out of the class lecture because you will make valuable "connections."

- The class lecture will be a "review," not an "introduction."

- You can ask better questions for clarification. (And impress your teacher!)

After you've practiced these steps for the first time, plan to spend five minutes "priming" your brain before reading a textbook. These simple strategies will make your comprehension skyrocket! In a short while, after some practice, your reading speed will double…or even triple! Do not underestimate the power of making connections!

How to Read Other Types of Texts

The steps on the previous two pages work best with textbooks, especially textbooks with a lot of visuals. But how can you apply these strategies to other types of texts and genres?

Use the Comprehension Model for Reading Other Types of Text

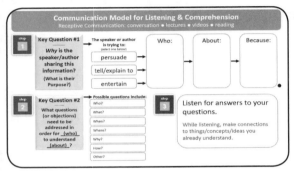

1. Identify the author's purpose for writing.

2. Brainstorm questions the text should answer.

3. Read to answer your questions. While reading, make connections to things, concepts, and ideas you already understand.

First, remember that the key to all learning – including reading comprehension – is to make connections! The most efficient and effective way to build connections…is by asking questions. So, let's go back to the Listening & Comprehension Model on page 89.

Additional tips for…

Nonfiction text, no visuals. Prime your
brain with some of the following strategies: Read the back of the book, read reviews on Amazon.com, do an Internet "image" search for the topic, and/or search for a summary of the text. Don't go overboard! Give yourself a strict time-limit, no more than 15 minutes. Most nonfiction includes headings and sub-headings, so continue turning them into questions, then reading to answer your questions.

Fiction. Fiction is often easier to comprehend than
nonfiction because we can better relate to "stories" than we can to facts about a previously unknown topic. However, many of the same strategies listed above are good for building background: read the back of the book, read reviews on Amazon.com, and search the Internet for a summary of the text. "Proper nouns" (names of characters and places) can get confusing. If you have trouble keeping track of these details, create a chart listing each person or place and details to remind you about each one's significance in the story.

Literature. Literature is "tricky" fiction. It's tricky because we
can usually relate to the elements and emotions of the story better than nonfiction. However, the problem is cutting through unfamiliar language and settings from unfamiliar times. Reviews on Amazon.com, text summaries, and video summaries can be very useful for building a framework for comprehension. Be prepared to look up unfamiliar words that can snag your understanding. As you read, make predictions about what you think will happen next to sharpen your comprehension.

What to Do When You Come to a Word You Don't Know

Step 1: Use context clues. Use the other words in the sentence to try to determine the meaning of the word you don't know.

Step 2: Take the word apart. Does the word contain any prefixes, roots, or suffixes that you can use to help you figure out what the word means?

Step 3: Look it up. If you can't figure out what the word is on your own, Google it!

Need to Learn New Vocabulary Words?

See "How to Study Vocabulary Words" at: www.StudySkills.com/bonus-edu.

When You Read, Do You See:

- Busy patterns of text or glare from the page?

- "Rivers of white" between words?

- Text that appears to move?

- Other "visual distortions"?

While you should always have your eyes checked for additional medical concerns, this may be a common situation that can be easily addressed. See "Visual Stress Syndrome" at: www.StudySkills.com/bonus-edu.

chapter 11
How to Take & Study Notes

The art of taking notes is more than simply writing information as a teacher is lecturing. It is about active listening (see Chapter 9). Active listening includes:

- Identifying important information.
- Writing down only key words/phrases so you don't miss other details.
- Knowing when you are "lost" and asking for clarification right away.

Listening Model

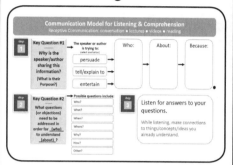

The three-step process for taking and studying notes follows the Listening Model... but in a different order.

Before Class...

step 1

Identify the purpose of the lecture.

The only way to learn new information is to connect it with something you already understand. Knowing the *purpose* of a lecture allows your brain to make connections with the information in lectures. The section in Chapter 9, "How to Be a Great Listener in Class," covers this in more detail.

However, there is an 80/20 Power Strategy to help you identify the purpose of a lecture, dramatically improving your attention, comprehension, and retention.

Read the Textbook Before Class!

The quickest and most effective way to understand a lecture is to read (or at least review) the textbook before class. Ask your teacher what sections of the text will be covered in the next lecture. Then, simply use the 80/20 Power Strategy for Reading, described in the previous chapter. This one strategy makes your reading *and* listening comprehension skyrocket!

Reading before class makes a great "Teacher Talking Point," because reading the text before class will allow you to contribute to class discussions and ask thoughtful questions.

Reading before class makes everything less "boring!" It helps the time pass more quickly, makes tests and homework easier, and simplifies your life. How can you *not* do it?

During Class…

 Open your textbook during lectures. The images and captions will continue to help you make valuable connections while your teacher is talking. (This tip is especially important if you were not able to read the text before class.)

step 3

Listen for connections. Write important details.

(Yes, skip ahead to "Step 3" on the Listening Model, when taking notes. We'll come back to Step 2 "after class.")

As you listen, make connections between the lecture and text. Even better, make personal connections to things you already know.

Write as if you are texting. You are the only person who will need to read your notes. Write fast using the same abbreviations you would use when texting a friend.

Draw visuals. Visuals are very brain-friendly! Draw as many diagrams, pictures, or doodles as you can…so long as they connect to the content.

Taking Notes Electronically?

The same three steps for note-taking apply whether you are writing or typing your notes.

See a video on how to format notes electronically at: www.StudySkills.com/bonus-edu.

Notes on Taking Notes

Oct. 18

- Date every page

Why date every page?

- Helps determine what information will be on specific tests/quizzes.
- Keeps papers in order in the event your binder "pops" open.

- Fold the left 1/3 of the paper

Why fold the left 1/3 of the paper?

- Write notes on right 2/3 of the paper.

- Create summary questions on the left side, as demonstrated on this page. (No more than 5 questions per page).

Why create summary questions?

* Turning your notes into questions helps you learn information at a higher level and therefore remember it better.
* The questions become an instant study guide.

- Take notes when a teacher...

- Says "This will be on the test." (Put a * next to it!)

- Says "This is an important point..."

- Writes information on the board.

Keep the back pages of the notebook paper open for adding additional information, drawing charts, pictures, symbols for your notes, etc.

Notes are easier to read and study when information is not crammed on each page. Give yourself some space to add additional information. Don't be stingy on the paper when you are taking notes...there are better ways to save trees. (You can recycle your notes when the class is over.)

Oct. 18

- Take notes when a teacher (cont.):

- Repeats the same information twice.

- Slows down as she speaks, giving you time to write.

When should I take notes?

- Talks with exaggerated hand gestures.

- Explains the same concept in several different ways.

- Says, "This is not in your textbook, but it is important..."

- Other Considerations:

- When possible, draw visuals (sketches, diagrams, charts, symbols) as you take notes.

What are some other things I can do when taking notes?

- If you miss something, draw a blank line as a place holder and clarify later.

- Keep it short. Write as little as possible.

- Use the same abbreviations you use for texting and create a few more of your own; your notes only have to make sense to you!

- Use as much space as you need to create clear notes for yourself.

After Class…

Create questions.

Reread your notes within 24 hours after class. As you read, fill in any details you remember but did not have time to write down. If something is confusing, make a note to ask your teacher to clarify the next day. Then…

Create summary questions, just like Jeopardy™. Your notes are the "answers." Now it's time to create the questions! The process of creating questions makes connections in your brain: you'll immediately shift into High-Gear Learning and will learn the information instantly. No more memorizing.

Your questions become an instant study guide! Save hours of study time for quizzes and tests: review notes simply by answering the questions you created! Reread your notes out loud.

*STUDY TIP: Take Ten. Every night, when you first sit down to start you homework, take TEN minutes to:

> **1. Organize your papers.** Check your binder and book bag. (2 minutes)
> **2. Review your notes.** Read through the notes you took earlier in the day. Write your "Jeopardy" questions. (8 minutes)

This routine can cut your homework time in <u>half!</u>

Studying Math Notes

Many students do not understand what it means to "study" for a math test. *Studying* brings to mind images of reading and memorizing a lot of notes. But this is not practical for math. Most of your math notes will actually come from your *homework*.

Studying for a math test includes:

- studying the vocabulary.
- doing your homework.
- paying attention to corrections made in class.

It also means learning from mistakes and doing practice problems to prepare for a test.

Studying for math tests begins with doing the homework. The information on the next page correlates with the math assignment on page 113. This assignment represents a typical piece of homework you might have to do in math. Although the types of problems may be different from your current math work, the concepts apply to nearly all forms of math assignments.

> **SOAR® Binder Tip**
>
> Use a tabbed divider behind your math folder to separate class notes from homework pages.

The numbers below correspond to the same symbols on the next page.

1 **Label the assignment.** *Always* put the page number and problem numbers at the top of the page.

2 **Each assignment = new page.** Use plenty of space to *neatly* do your work. Keep place values aligned properly so that all digits in the ones place, tens place, etc. align. Math teachers will confirm that many points are lost on math tests by students who cannot read their own writing and end up confusing themselves!

3 **Remain calm.** If you encounter a problem that you do not know how to do, don't panic. Look at the lesson in your book to see if you can figure out how to do the problem. If, after three minutes, you can't figure it out, circle the problem number, record it at the top of the page, and *move on.* Continue to skip any problems that you can't figure out and come back to them once you have completed all of the problems that you *can* do.

4 **Try each problem.** However, if you get to the end of the assignment and only have a few problems that you cannot answer, leave them. Ask your teacher about them the next day. If you cannot figure out the majority of the assignment, then you need to ask for help from your parent(s), a neighbor, your teacher, or an in-school tutor.

5 **Ask your teacher.** Most teachers begin math class by correcting homework from the night before. When she asks, "Are there any questions from last night's homework?" raise your hand and get your questions answered. (This helps build rapport with your teacher, too.)

6 **Study Guide = "problem" problems.** When it is time to prepare for a test, go back through the homework and redo the problems with which you had trouble.

Conclusion

These simple steps help you learn the material *throughout* a chapter or unit, rather than cramming the night before a test. (Cramming is nearly impossible in math). A few simple steps while doing your math homework will make class time more valuable, save you a lot of study time, and help you score higher on tests.

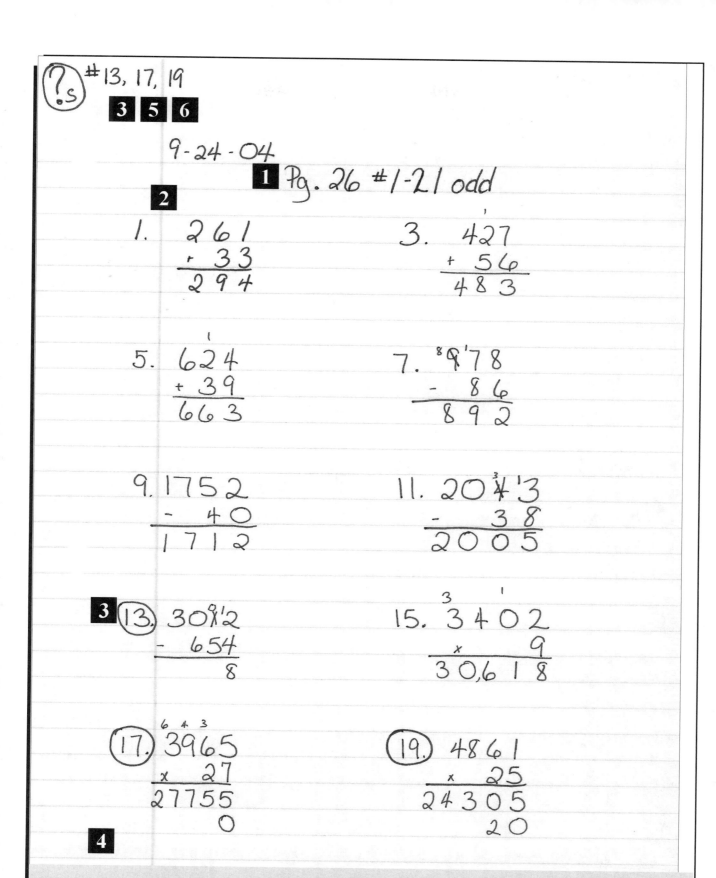

?s #13, 17, 19

3 **5** **6**

9-24-04

1 Pg. 26 #1-21 odd

2

1. 261
   + 33
   ‾‾‾‾‾
    294

3. 427
   + 56
   ‾‾‾‾‾
    483

5. 624
   + 39
   ‾‾‾‾‾
    663

7. 978
   - 86
   ‾‾‾‾‾
    892

9. 1752
   - 40
   ‾‾‾‾‾
    1712

11. 2043
    - 38
   ‾‾‾‾‾‾
     2005

3 (13.) 3012
       - 654
      ‾‾‾‾‾‾
          8

15. 3402
    ×   9
   ‾‾‾‾‾‾‾
    30,618

(17.) 3965
      × 27
     ‾‾‾‾‾‾‾
      27755
          0

(19.) 4861
      × 25
     ‾‾‾‾‾‾‾
      24305
         20

4

chapter 12
How to Take Tests

☐ **Do you ever get nervous when taking a test?**

☐ **Does the thought of studying for tests ever feel overwhelming?**

☐ **Have you ever been disappointed with your score on a test after you worked hard to prepare for it?**

☐ **Do you ever feel like there *has* to be a better way to prepare for and perform on tests?**

There *is* a better way…

As with everything else, there are a few tricks and tips for making test preparation and test-taking more efficient. The test on the next two pages will assess your test-taking I.Q. and give you some clues about good strategies to use. Try the test first, then read the Answer Key, beginning on page 118 to correct your answers and identify hidden clues within each question.

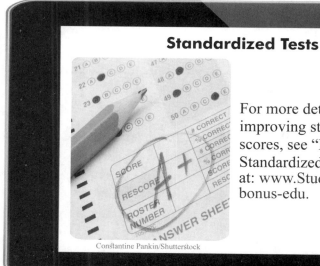

Standardized Tests

For more details on improving standardized test scores, see "How to Improve Standardized Test Scores" at: www.StudySkills.com/bonus-edu.

Constantine Pankin/Shutterstock

The Test Test

Directions: At the end of each statement, write True or False on the blank line. Ignore the "correct statement" line until after you have read the answer key.

① Most of your test-preparation is done when you take notes, read the text, and develop questions about both. _____

Correct statement:

_____

_____

② You should throw away all of your work as soon as it is checked or graded because it will only clutter up your folders. _____

Correct statement:

_____

_____

③ Getting a good night's sleep and eating a healthy breakfast are more beneficial than cramming all night the night before a test. _____

Correct statement:

_____

_____

④ When you are undecided about a test answer, your first hunch is usually right. _____

Correct statement:

_____

_____

⑤ It is important to be the first person done with the test because that means that you aced the test. _____

Correct statement:

_____

_____

Continue ➔

The Test Test
continued

Multiple choice: Underline the best answer for each question.

⑥ The best way to study for a test is:
    A. Spend a few solid hours of non-stop studying the night before a test.
    B. Do your reading and homework on time and review your notes for a few minutes every day.
    C. Highlight any questions that you have on any of your work or notes so that you remember to ask them in class.
    D. Both B and C.

⑦ Preparing a study guide…
    A. Should be based only on what the teacher tells you about the test.
    B. Is automatically done for you when you use the questioning technique for taking notes and reading.
    C. Means spending many hours, the night before the test, rewriting all of your notes.
    D. Only needs to be done for big tests, such as final exams.

⑧ When your teacher gives you a study guide, you should:
    A. Ignore it because you have already made your own study guide from your notes.
    B. Use it to help you decipher what to focus on the night or two before the test.
    C. Toss your notes and textbook aside; the study guide is all you need.
    D. Stop paying attention in class. The study guide has all the answers you will need for the test.

⑨ The night before a test, you should:
    A. Look over your work for a minute. You don't need to spend any more time on it because you've taken notes and done your homework.
    B. Spend a few solid hours studying, non-stop.
    C. Spend 30-60 minutes reviewing your notes, homework, and text, and quizzing yourself by talking out loud.
    D. None of the above.

⑩ To study for a final exam or unit test, your best option is to:
    A. Study corrected tests from the semester.
    B. Reread every chapter covered since the beginning of the semester.
    C. Forget studying. You either know it or you don't.
    D. None of the above.

STOP ●

The Test Test
ANSWER KEY

Now that you have completed the test, check your answers below and find additional hints for taking tests.

<u>Directions</u>: At the end of each statement, write True or False in the blank line. Ignore the "correct statement" line until after you have read the answer key.

Did you notice the statement in the directions that told you to *ignore* the "correct statement line" until after you read the answer key?

On any given test, 50% of students will not read the directions. If this was a real test and you did not follow these directions, you would have lost points already.

Lesson: Pay attention to the directions!

① Most of your test-preparation is done when you take notes, read the text, and develop questions about both. <u>TRUE</u>

Hint:

The word "most" is an indication that this answer is probably true. Any time a T/F question has a word such as "some," "most," "few," etc. the answer is probably true. Conversely, most questions that have words like "all" or "none" are likely to be false because very few things are that definitive.

② You should throw away all of your work as soon as it is checked or graded because it will only clutter up your folders. <u>FALSE</u>

Correct Statement:

Old assignments, especially old tests/quizzes, are the most valuable study guides you can have for final exams or unit tests. Do not throw anything away until you have received your final grade in case your teacher made a computational mistake. If your binder is getting overloaded, transfer papers to your Home Paper Station.

③ Getting a good night's sleep and eating a healthy breakfast are more beneficial than cramming all night the night before a test. <u>TRUE</u>

Hint:

Good sleep and proper nutrition will keep you alert and help prevent "stupid" mistakes. Drowsy drivers have been shown to demonstrate similar behavior on the road to some drunk drivers, illustrating how impaired your thinking and reasoning can be when you are tired.

④ When you are undecided about a test answer, your first hunch is usually right. <u>TRUE</u>

Hint:

If you are truly stuck and have no clue about an answer, go with whatever answer first seemed most appropriate to you. Chances are that your subconscious, long-term memory is working on your behalf, but is simply lacking the proper recall to help you clarify the answer.

⑤ It is important to be one of the first people done with the test because that means that you aced the test. <u>FALSE</u>

Correct Statement:

There is no such thing as a stupid question, but there is such a thing as a *stupid* answer. Those are the items that, after your test has been graded, make you think, "OHHH! I knew that!" The best way to avoid *stupid* mistakes is to take the time to reread your test when you are done. Use all the time you have. It is a little frustrating trying to concentrate after you have completed the test, but *every point counts*. If you reread your tests regularly, you will likely find and correct an error more than 50% of the time!

<u>Multiple choice</u>: Underline the best answer for each question.

Did you notice that the instructions told you to <u>underline</u> the answer? Little details in the directions like this are commonly overlooked by students. Sometimes, these omissions can cost points from the final score.

⑥ The best way to study for a test is:
   A. Spend a few solid hours of non-stop studying the night before a test.
   B. Do your reading and homework on time and review your notes for a few minutes every day.
   C. Highlight any questions that you have on any of your work or notes so that you remember to ask them in class.
   D. <u>Both B and C</u>.

Hint:

Teachers like to cram a lot of information into questions. Any time you see more than one option combined together, such as "All of the above," or "Both B & C," that answer is *likely* to be correct.

⑦ Preparing a study guide...
   A. Should be based only on what the teacher tells you about the test.
   B. <u>Is automatically done for you when you use the questioning technique for taking notes and reading textbooks.</u>
   C. Means spending many hours, the night before the test, rewriting all of your notes.
   D. Only needs to be done for big tests, such as final exams.

Hint:

If you have no other clue to figure out an answer, then choose the longest answer...it is usually the correct choice.

⑧ When your teacher gives you a study guide, you should:
   A. Ignore it because you have already made your own study guide from your notes.
   B. <u>Use it to help you decipher what to focus on the night or two before the test.</u>
   C. Toss your notes and textbook aside; the study guide is all you need.
   D. Stop paying attention in class. The study guide has all the answers you will need for the test.

Hint:

If possible, avoid being absent the day or two before a test. Valuable test information is usually given at this time.

⑨ The night before a test, you should:
  A. Look over your work for a minute. You don't need to spend any more time on it because you've taken notes and done your homework.
  B. Spend a few solid hours studying non-stop.
  C. <u>Spend 30-60 minutes reviewing your notes, homework, and textbook, then quiz yourself by talking out loud.</u>
  D. None of the above.

Hint:

If you have consistently been doing homework and reviewing notes, then 30-60 minutes reviewing and making final connections the night before a test should be all you need. This preparation will also give you valuable confidence before a test.

⑩ To study for a final exam or unit test, your best option is to:
  A. <u>Study corrected tests from the semester.</u>
  B. Reread every chapter covered since the beginning of the semester.
  C. Forget studying. You either know it or you don't.
  D. None of the above.

Hint:

Who has time for "B"? The answer is clearly "A" because teachers do not have a lot of time to create brand new questions for end-of-semester (or end-of-unit) tests. Therefore, they usually pull questions from previous tests and quizzes for their final exams.

Your Score:
——— out of 10

If you scored:

⊙ **9-10**…Congratulations, you are a test-taking champ!

⊙ **6-8**…You have a good start. Practice a couple of the strategies in this chapter to improve your test performance.

⊙ **1-5**…Reread the chapter and select three or four strategies you can begin practicing right away. In a month, try two more.

Review Graded Tests

Mistakes are one of the most powerful learning tools. Reviewing graded tests is an excellent way to continue learning. Obviously, this process will not improve the immediate test grade, but it does improve long-term learning, final exam grades, and standardized test scores.

More Test-Taking Tips

The Test Test provides many hints and guidelines for taking tests. However, there are some other tips to consider:

A⁺ **Have a watch or clock available when taking a test.** Proper pacing is important when taking a test. A day or two before the test, ask your teacher how much time you will have and how many questions will be on the test.

A⁺ **Before you answer any questions, quickly read every question on the test.** There are two benefits to this:

1) You will see the whole test and be better able to judge how much time to spend on each question or section.

2) Clues for some answers are often included in other questions, so you will likely find new answers.

A⁺ **If you get to a question that you don't know, don't waste your time and energy; mark the question, skip it, and move on.** Go back to that question after you complete the rest of the test. Otherwise, you will waste a lot of time and build up anxiety that could cause you to lose focus on the rest of the test.

A⁺ **When you first receive a test, immediately write down any information you needed to memorize, such as formulas, specific dates, names, etc.** Write this down right away, before forgetting important information.

Multiple Choice Questions

A⁺ After reading the question, try to think of the correct answer *before* you read your options.

A⁺ Read all answers first. Sometimes, item "A" will *sound* correct, but item "C" may end up being more appropriate.

A+ Cross out items that you know are wrong and then choose your answer from the remaining options.

A+ Answers with phrases like "all of the above" and "both a & b" are likely to be the correct choices, but only use this clue if you are stuck.

A+ The longest answers are also likely to be the correct choices, but again, only use this clue if you do not know the answer for sure.

Fill-in-the-Blank Questions

A+ Look for grammar clues that may give hints, such as the word "an," that will indicate that the answer begins with a vowel, or something that indicates a plural word, past tense verb, etc.

A+ Sometimes the length and/or number of blanks may be a hint.

A+ After you have filled in the blank, reread the statement with your answer to make sure that your answer makes sense in the sentence.

Essay Questions

A+ In the margin, write a brief outline of the major points you want to include in your answer. This will help you write an organized, logical, and concise answer. Teachers do not want to read lengthy responses. They prefer short and to-the-point answers. In fact, many teachers may *only* read your outline when grading your paper. An outline may also help you get partial credit if you run out of time.

A+ Begin your answer by restating the question. Remember, get to the point quickly.

A+ Write neatly. It is definitely *not* to your advantage to frustrate your teacher!

Conclusion

This chapter includes several tips for improving performance on tests. However, the single best way to prepare for tests is to read your textbooks, regularly review notes, and learn from your homework assignments and quizzes. Following these steps will ensure that you have a solid grasp of the information and will have no problems acing any test!

chapter 13
How to Write Papers

Never Be Intimidated by Writing Again!

Know your purpose for writing. People struggle to write primarily when they are not clear about their purpose for writing. Once you have clearly defined your purpose, all writing – from short emails to a 300-page book – is simply a process of answering questions.

The Communication Model for Speaking & Writing guides you through this process.

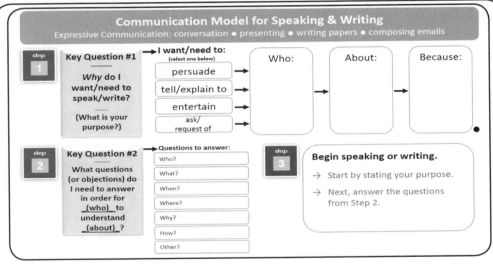

1. Define your purpose for writing.
2. Brainstorm questions you need to answer to achieve your purpose.
3. Answer the questions.

"How Do I Use This Model to Write a Paper?"

The following pages show how the three steps from The Writing Model apply to writing papers. The first example is a template you can use to write a book report. The next example shows how to write a research paper. But the research doesn't have to be intimidating either. My 3-D Graphic Organizer will help you help you find and organize your research easily, so you can write your report quickly and painlessly. Take a look…

Example: How to Use the Writing Model for a Book Report

Assignment: Book Report

step 1
 	
Define your purpose.
	I need to <u>explain to</u> <u>my teacher</u> <u>about what happened in the</u>
	    (expression type) (who) (about)
	<u>book and what I learned</u> <u>because my teacher needs to confirm</u>
	                             (because)
	<u>my understanding.</u>

step 2a **Make a list of questions.** Key question: *"What questions do I need to answer in order for my teacher to understand what I learned?"*	1. Who are the main characters? 2. What happens in the story? 3. Where does this story take place? 4. What is the title? 5. Who is the author? 6. When does this story take place? 7. What is the moral or the theme? 8. Who is the hero? Villain? 9. How did the setting affect the story? 10. How does this story relate to things I've experienced? 11. How does this story relate to other books I've read? 12. What is the plot of the story? 13. Who solves the problem?
step 2b **Create categories by grouping similar questions together.**	1. What are some general pieces of information that are needed to introduce the book? (4, 5, 12) 2. Who are the main characters? Describe them. (1, 8) 3. Where does the story take place? What makes the setting unique and special for the story? (3, 6, 9) 4. What problems did the characters encounter? How did they resolve the problem? (2, 13) 5. What is my conclusion? (7, 10, 11) Note: The numbers in ( ) at the end of each question show items from Step 2a that were grouped into categories.
step 3 **Start writing. Simply answer the questions.**	To write your paper, simply answer each of the questions listed above. The answer for each question creates a concise paragraph. This procedure helps you create an organized paper with well-defined paragraphs.

NOTE: Teachers usually provide the "categories" when they assign a paper. In that case, you simply need to turn the categories into questions. See the next page for an example.

How to Write a Research Report

Most writing assignments list the sub-topics you need to address. For example, the assignment on the next page is actually given to ninth-grade students at my local high school. It lists several sub-topics the report is expected to cover.

How to Do Online Research & Verify Sources

How do you find trusted resources online? See our guide, "How to Do Online Research & Verify Sources" at: www.StudySkills.com/bonus-edu.

These sub-topics can easily be turned into questions. The answers to each question will become paragraphs for your report. These questions will then guide your research.

The chart below will guide you through the process of converting these sub-topics into questions. The 3-D Organizer on the following page will help you organize these questions and your research notes, almost effortlessly, to produce a high-quality paper.

<u>Directions:</u> Practice creating questions from the topics listed on the next page. The first three have been done as examples:

Assigned Sub-Topic:	Becomes a Question:
Introductory Paragraph	Are there any interesting points, stories, quotes,statistics, etc., that I may want to use as I introduce the topic of my paper?
Education/Skills	What skills and education are required for this career?
Description of the Work	What types of duties are required of this career?
Location & Setting	
Salary (Compensation)	
Closing Paragraph	

Career Research Report

Assignment: Research and write a report about a career that is of interest to you. Choosing a career is an important decision because it will determine how you spend a significant portion of your life. This assignment will help you learn more about a potential career for your future.

I. Report Guidelines

Your paper must be approximately 2-4 pages in length and include a Works Cited page.

II. Report Contents

Your report must address the following topics:

A. Opening Paragraph

Capture my attention with one or two interesting points, stories, quotes, statistics, etc. This paragraph should briefly describe the topic of your paper.

B. Education/Skills

Describe what type of education and/or training is required for this career, including specific types of degrees or certifications. Explain special skills and personality traits that are well-suited for this career.

C. Description of the Work

Give a general description of the duties required by this career and describe a typical day on the job.

D. Location & Setting

Some careers are highly concentrated in certain parts of the country. Describe general locations where jobs in your field are located, the type of community you might live in, and the type of environment in which you would work (medical, office, travel, working from home, etc.).

E Salary/Compensation

Indicate what you expect to make in this career, including beginning wages, average income, and salary cap (the most you can make).

F. Closing Paragraph

Conclude your report with a summary about this career and a brief statement describing your opinion of this career, now that you have researched more details about it.

3-D Research Report Organizer

This tool is amazingly effective for organizing your writing into logical, cohesive paragraphs. This technique has been used by students of all ages, from 3rd graders to college students, and it transforms writing skills *instantly*. In fact, I used a variation of this technique to write my 50-page Master's Thesis (see page 136 for more details). This is truly one strategy I wish I had known much earlier in life!

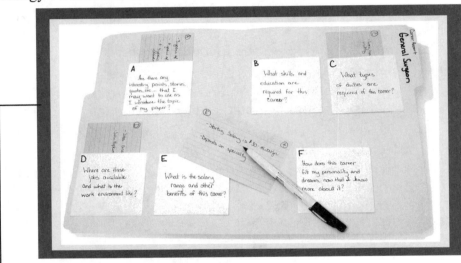

This 3-Dimensional writing tool helps keep all notes, thoughts, and memos in a logical order.

Materials Needed

- ❑ 1 file folder
- ❑ 3 or 4 envelopes (size 6: $3\frac{5}{8} x 6\frac{1}{2}$")
- ❑ 12-30 index cards (3 x 5")
- ❑ Glue
- ❑ Pen or marker
- ❑ Scissors
- ❑ Copy of the *Report Planning Guide* from www.StudySkills.com/bonus-edu. (Optional, but helpful for the first time you use this tool.)

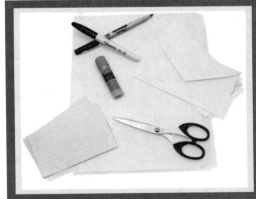

Directions for Assembly

1○

Seal the envelopes shut, then cut them in half to form pockets. You will need one pocket for each paragraph of your report.

2○

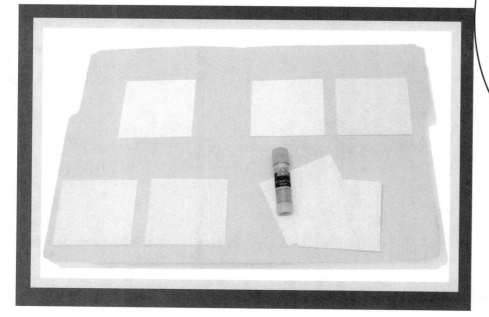

Glue the halved envelopes onto the inside surface of your file folder, as pictured. Make sure the opening of the pocket is towards the *top* of the folder.

3°

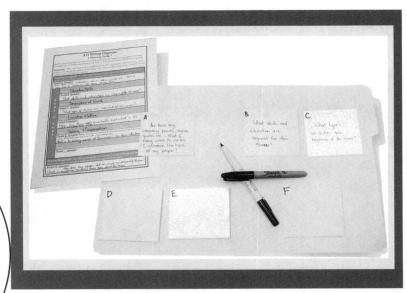

Label each pocket in alphabetical order. Use the Writing Planning Guide (www.StudySkills.com/bonus-edu) to determine the questions each paragraph will answer. Record one question on each pocket.

4°

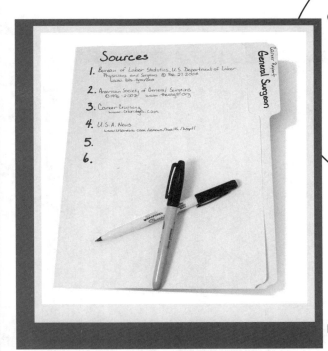

On the front cover of your folder, list all sources you will use for your research, including encyclopedias, magazines, websites, and books. Number each source.

5○

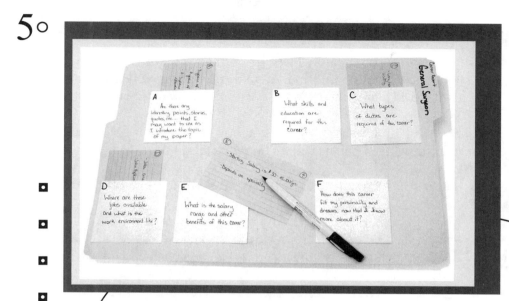

Start your research. As you find an answer for each question, record the answer on an index card.

To avoid plagiarism, write your answers in your own words and record the page number of the source where the information was found. If you believe using a direct quote is best, be sure to put quotations around the text that you copy on your index card.

6○

In the upper left corner of each card, record the pocket letter in which the card belongs. On the right-hand corner, write the source number for each card.

Once your research is complete, it's time to start writing. See the next page for more details on creating your paper.

Writing the First Draft

Once you have approximately three to five index cards for each pocket, you should have enough information to begin writing your paper. (You may not have as many notes for the opening and closing paragraphs.)

The following directions will show you how to turn your note cards into a clear, well-organized paper. See a sample paper on page 135.

See a sample paper on page 135.

1° Introduce the purpose; write the opening paragraph.

You may not have many (or any) notes for this paragraph because it is an overview of the paper. Include interesting points, stories, statistics, or quotes to hook your reader's attention. It is often easier to write this paragraph *last*, after all of the other paragraphs have been written.

2° Check index cards from the first pocket.

Make sure they all answer the question for that specific pocket.

3° Arrange the cards in the most logical order.

Imagine you are explaining the information to someone in a conversation. This strategy will not only help you figure out the order, but it will also help you with step 4.

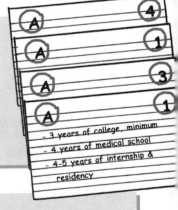

- 3 years of college, minimum
- 4 years of medical school
- 4-5 years of internship & residency

4° Write the paragraph.

If you were careful to fill out your note cards in your own words, then you can mostly copy your note cards. However, to make the language sound natural, use the tip from Step 3: imagine you are telling the information to someone else. This approach will help your writing transition from one detail to another without sounding like a list of facts.

Have "Writer's Block?"

Pretend you are writing an email to a friend. Stephen King says, "All novels are really letters aimed at one person." The truth is, *all writing* should be written so the reader feels as if you wrote just to him or her. Even academic writing should be written as if you are explaining your topic to one person. Using a conversational tone makes all writing easier to understand, *especially* when writing about a complicated topic.

5○ Repeat steps 2-4 for the remaining paragraphs.

6○ Write a closing paragraph.

Closing paragraphs summarize the main idea of the report and often contain a short statement about your personal thoughts, comments, or observations about the topic. The closing paragraph will often connect to a fact or comment written in the opening paragraph.

7○ Revise your paper.

Revising is about making sure that your paper makes sense and "sounds" good! Do all sentences flow together and make sense? Do the paragraphs make sense and transition nicely from one to another? Revising checklists are a nice tool to use for this phase of the writing process. It is always a good idea to ask an adult to help you revise as well.

8○ Finally, edit your paper.

Use spell check and grammar check on the computer, but never rely on them completely. Check your own paper for misspellings, typos, correct grammar, etc. Then ask someone else to double-check your paper for spelling and grammar as well.

Revising and Editing Checklist

Download a revision checklist at:
www.StudySkills.com/bonus-edu.

These note cards were used to write the highlighted paragraph on page 135.

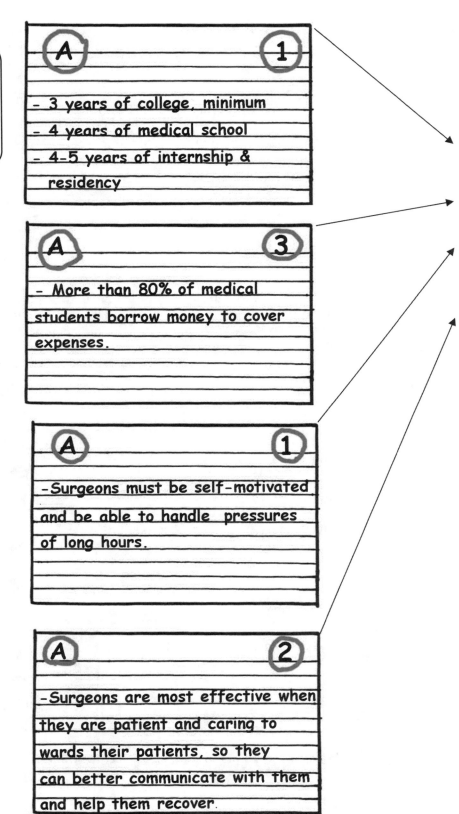

A   **1**

- 3 years of college, minimum
- 4 years of medical school
- 4-5 years of internship & residency

A   **3**

- More than 80% of medical students borrow money to cover expenses.

A   **1**

-Surgeons must be self-motivated and be able to handle pressures of long hours.

A   **2**

-Surgeons are most effective when they are patient and caring towards their patients, so they can better communicate with them and help them recover.

Name: *Julia R.*

General Surgeon

A surgeon not only puts her mind and hands on the job, but also her heart. In many cases, the difference between life and death rests in her hands. As a general surgeon, I would have the opportunity to help other people in a very meaningful way and would also be able to stay active, instead of sitting at a desk all day.

To become a surgeon, there is an extensive amount of education and training required. First, surgeons must complete at least three years of college. Afterwards, they are required to attend four years of medical school and then participate in an internship and residency, which could take up to five years. The training is not cheap, either! More than 80% of medical students borrow money to cover their expenses while in school. Surgeons must be self-motivated and able to handle pressures of long hours on the job. The most effective surgeons are people who are patient and caring towards their patients. These traits allow them to communicate with their patients to help them recover better.

The nature of work that a surgeon does will depend on his/her specialty. Most surgeons will specialize in a specific area such as cardiology, orthopedics, or oncology, to name a few. Regardless of specialty, however, surgeons can usually count on long hours. Most work 60 or more hours per week in hospitals, clinics, or other private practices. These hours are often split between office consultations and the operating room.

Some of the most highly trained surgeons in the country work in the top three research and patient care facilities in the United States: Johns Hopkins in Baltimore, Mayo Clinic in Rochester, MN, and Massachusetts General Hospital in Boston. However, most surgeons are likely to find work in any part of the country, particularly in more urban areas. Surgeons do not typically travel for work, except when they attend out-of-town medical seminars for further training. Otherwise, the only travel surgeons take is on vacation, which is typically 20-30 vacation days per year.

All of the expenses for medical school may be worth it when you consider the salaries some surgeons make. The average salary is approximately $340,000. While a starting salary is $30,000-$45,000 a year, earning potential grows rapidly. Earnings usually depend on how many patients a surgeon sees and the types of procedures she performs.

There are many pros and cons to working in the medical field. Overall, however, I think I would enjoy being able to help people, even help save lives. Despite the long hours and expensive training, I would certainly sacrifice some things to save others; I want to touch the hearts of other people in life. If I were a patient that had to undergo surgery, I would certainly want a surgeon with this level of compassion.

Each paragraph in the career research paper on the previous page answers the questions that were created on page 126. Creating questions before you write significantly helps you focus your research and keep your paragraphs on topic.

The 3-D Research Report Organizer: Electronic Version

andersphoto/Shutterstock

You can apply the concept of the 3-D Organizer on the computer. This option is best if you have a large paper to write, or simply prefer to type. (The computerized version is optimal for papers longer than eight paragraphs.)

You should use the file-folder at least *once* before using a computerized version. Moving and organizing the note cards with your hands will help your brain internalize the organization process so it will feel very natural to use again in the future – with another file-folder *or* with the computer.

To modify the 3-D Organizer on a computer, follow these steps:

1○ Open your word processor program. Create a "New Folder" and give it the same title as your paper.

2○ Create a new document within this folder for each question you need to answer. (The computer documents replace the envelope pockets.) The title of each document will be the question that you would have written on the pockets in your file folder.

3○ As you find answers to each question, simply click on the corresponding document and type the information in a bullet-point list (instead of filling out individual index cards). Be sure to include the source for each answer you add to the list.

4○ When your research is done, print each document. Use the answers on each document to write your first draft. For longer papers, your "question documents" may represent separate sections in your paper, instead of paragraphs.

How to Write an Email

All nonfiction writing is about "answering questions," usually before the questions have ever been asked. The process of answering questions applies to writing emails, too. See "How to Write an Email" at: www.StudySkills.com/bonus-edu.

chapter 14
How to Give a Presentation

"Speaking in public" is often ranked as people's top fear! It used to be mine. I was very shy as a child and teen. But when I had to give a speech in 8th grade, my dad was determined that I would conquer my fear.

My dad is a gifted speaker and presenter. It was intimidating to work with him. He made me practice and practice and practice…. Just when I thought I couldn't take any more, he really pushed me out of my comfort zone, making me stand on a table in our front room to practice my speech. (It was dark out, so the room was lit up like a fish bowl from the busy street outside.)

He ran to the back of the house and yelled, "Do it again!" I felt ridiculous yelling my speech so Dad could hear it: across the front room, through the kitchen, down the hall, and into the back room. "Louder!" he yelled back. "One more time." "I can't hear you!" "Again…."

Finally, I passed his test! He gave me a hug and sent me off to bed. I doubt I returned the favor; I was not happy.

I gave my speech the next day. To my surprise, I wasn't very nervous. After standing on a table awkwardly the night before, standing at a podium didn't seem so bad. I gave my speech and thought I did OK. But as the day went on, I got a compliment from almost every person in the class. People stopped me everywhere: in the hallway, at lunch, even in the restroom to say, "Hey, great speech today!" "Susan, you did a great job." Even the "cool" kids complimented me. That *never* happened.

Since that day, I have never been afraid to speak in public. Standing on the table in my living room, I never would have dreamed that my dad was giving me the greatest gift of my life; I now make a living speaking to students and parents, training teachers, creating videos and webinars, and doing radio/TV interviews.

Dad's lesson? Stand on a table and yell!

Well, not exactly. (But it wouldn't hurt.) What I really learned from Dad is the importance of *preparation.* To this day, I never go into a speech or interview "cold," even though I could probably give most speeches in my sleep. Preparation builds confidence.

Why Is Public Speaking So Difficult?

The problem is that most people don't understand the difference between spoken and written language. Knowing this difference is the key to giving an engaging presentation.

Spoken vs. Written Language: How Are They Different?

Written language is not just putting "spoken words" in print. Spoken and written language both use the same vocabulary and grammar structure. But as you learned in chapter 8, the vast majority of a spoken message is conveyed through tone of voice and body language.

Only 7% of spoken messages are delivered through words. Written language, however, relies *entirely* on words, so the words must be chosen with much more precision.

With spoken language, the speaker controls the speed of the message, but the listener can ask for clarification. With written language, the reader cannot ask for clarification. However, the reader can control the speed of reading and can reread a message as often as necessary for understanding.

The greatest difference lies in the amount of planning required to deliver the message. Most spoken language is casual and in response to the people, place, and time surrounding the conversation.

Since spoken language evaporates the moment it is uttered, there is usually very little, if any, planning involved. Since there is no planning, most spoken language uses simple words and inconsistent grammar. And since the listener can ask for clarification, even accuracy is a secondary consideration.

On the other hand, written language is permanent. So the writer usually gives more time to word choice, eliminating repetitive words/ideas, and properly adjusting grammar. The result is language that sounds much more formal than spoken language.

All of these differences lead to the two great challenges of public speaking:

> **1. To clearly communicate your message to an audience that cannot interrupt for clarification,** as it would during a conversation or when reading written text.

> **2. To give a presentation that sounds like natural speech,** even though it required a lot of planning, usually with notes in "print."

How to Overcome the Two Great Challenges of Public Speaking

1. *To clearly communicate your message to your audience…* Organize your content with the 3-D graphic organizer. Add visuals.

2. *To give a highly planned presentation that sounds like natural speech…* Practice your presentation. (Standing on tables is optional.)

Organize Your Content with a 3-D Graphic Organizer

Preparing content for a speech is very similar to preparing content for a writing assignment:

1○ **Know your purpose.** By now, you know this well. Knowing your purpose is critical for creating a clear and focused presentation.

2○ **Create your questions.** In many cases, your teacher will provide the topics; you will simply need to turn them into questions, as you did on page 126. Otherwise, refer back to the Speaking & Writing Model on page 88 for question prompts.

3○ **Create your 3-D organizer.** The 3-D organizer allows you to organize your thoughts in a clear and logical way. This clarity is essential for your audience!

4○ **Answer your questions.** This time, write phrases and key words only, instead of full sentences as you would do for a writing assignment. One answer per note card. Continue until you have three to four note cards per pocket. Label your note cards with the source number and pocket number, as illustrated on page 131.

5○ **Consider your opening and closing.** Do you have two pockets reserved for your opening statement and closing remarks? If possible, tell stories. Personal stories are the #1 secret to forming a bond with your audience. The opening, especially, is a great place to tell a story. (Just as I did at the beginning of this chapter.) Your closing usually circles back to the story from the beginning.

6○ **Check the index cards from the first pocket.** Make sure they all answer the question for that specific pocket.

7 **Arrange the cards in the most logical order.** To determine the best order, imagine you are explaining the information to someone in a conversation.

8 **Number your cards in order for quick and easy reference.** Apply the order number right next to the pocket letter. For example, all of the cards from pocket A will be labeled: "A-1," "A-2," "A-3," "A-4," etc.

9 **Repeat steps 6-8 for all remaining pockets.** Now that all of your content has been organized and collected, you are ready to add visuals.

How to Strategically Use:
Visuals, Props, & Digital Media

People remember only 20% of what they hear and only 30% of what they see. But they remember 50% of what they see *and* hear.[1] You can more than double the retention of your audience by adding visuals!

1 **Determine appropriate visuals,** including photos/illustrations, props, or multi-media resources.
- Have at least one visual *per pocket* of your 3-D organizer. A good rule-of-thumb is to change visuals every 20 to 40 seconds. Add more as necessary.
- Select visuals that somehow represent an answer to the question you recorded on the pocket of your 3-D organizer.

2 **If creating a slide show, select a clean template.**
- The background should be subtle, with high contrast. (Light background with dark text *or* dark background with light text.)
- Fonts should be simple and easy to read. Helvetica or Arial is best. Font size ranges from 18 to 48-point for slide presentations.

3 **Create your title slide.** This will include:
- The title of your presentation and
- Your name, as the presenter.

[1]Metcalf, T. (1997) Listening to your clients, Life Association News, 92(7) p16 - 18

4○ Create your slides: Minimum of one slide per pocket.

- The headline of the slide can be the question on your pocket. Or use a few keywords from the question to create the headline.

- After your headline, no more than six words per slide. You want your audience listening to you, not reading your slide.

- No more than two visuals per slide. If you need more slides to "answer this question," use additional slides with the same headline. Empty space enhances readability.

- No fancy transitions. They are distracting.

5○ Test your slide presentation.

- Do the slides match the order of your pockets and note cards?

- Does everything show up as you expect?

- Did you check grammar and spelling?

6○ Now, it's time to *practice*!

How to Practice a Presentation

The best public speakers don't memorize their speech; they simply know their topic so well that they can speak about it very naturally. The goal of your practice sessions is to become so comfortable with the content, timing, visuals, and technology that when you are actually presenting, you can focus on *connecting with the audience*.

Toastmasters International is the leading authority on public speaking. They are a global organization that has been training people in public speaking skills for over 90 years.

They coach people to focus on one specific element of the speaking process with each practice session and speech. That's what you should do. The list on the next page can look a little daunting, but focus on one item every time you practice your speech. Your confidence will grow with each round of practice.

How to Practice a Presentation (Continued)

1. **Practice out loud, standing up, with visuals and props.** You're just getting warmed up.

2. **Practice with variety.** With each practice, use different words. Share your message like you are talking to a friend.

3. **Practice your "non-verbals";** confident posture, hands relaxed, smiling…making eye-contact. (For now, you have to make eye-contact with furniture and stuffed animals. Just practice.)

4. **Practice for timing.** Insert planned pauses to emphasize a point, or when you expect a reaction from the audience. "Pauses" will feel like an eternity from the front of a room, but don't rush through them.

5. **Give your opening special attention.** Getting started is the most challenging part of the whole presentation. Once you're off to a good start, the rest will flow.

6. **Practice in front of a real audience.** Grab your mom, kid brother, and the family dog. It is often more uncomfortable practicing in front of the people you know best than it is to give a public speech. It's almost like standing on a table in the middle of a room. It pushes you out of your comfort zone a bit.

7. **Record your speech on video.** Nothing is more objective than seeing your own performance on video. Watch for each of the elements above and pick two things to improve.

8. **Now you're ready to go!** You've got a well-organized presentation and you're fully prepared to deliver it. You should rock and roll. But, what if you don't? What if you say the wrong thing or forget a word? Just go with it! Say something like, "Excuse me, I was mistaken. I meant to say…" If you're *really* nervous, be honest with your audience and say so; that's the quickest way to drain your anxiety. Amazingly, it will help you bond with your audience, too. They want you to succeed!

chapter 15
How to Use Language Resources

What "language" skills do you need in college and the workplace? The Common Core College and Career Readiness Anchor Standards have identified six specific skill areas. Below you will find information and links for resources that *real* people use in the *real* world when they encounter a language question or challenge.

Grammar Conventions of English

After years of diagramming sentences, are you still confused about the various parts of speech?

1. Clarify your confusion quickly with simple symbols. See "Grammar Symbols" at: www.StudySkills.com/bonus-edu.

2. Master the most common mistakes. See the "Most Common Language Errors" at: www.StudySkills.com/bonus-edu.

Capitalization, Punctuation, and Spelling

In the professional world, poor capitalization, punctuation, and/or spelling sends the message that you don't pay attention to details. Follow these simple rules with all of your writing:

1. *Always* reread emails before you send them. Use spell-check and grammar-check.

2. *Always* have one or two other people review important reports, documents, or articles before you submit or publish your final draft. We can't trust our own eyes to catch all our errors.

3. Master the most common mistakes. See the "Most Common Language Errors" at: www.StudySkills.com/bonus-edu.

Know Your Language!

In college and the workplace, you are expected to use language effectively in a variety of settings. (Obviously!) This skill is also known as "syntax." People of all ages use games, such as the popular "brain games," to build their language skills. Find links to popular language games at: www. StudySkills.com/bonus-edu.

Don't Know a Word?

We all come across words we've never seen before. What do professionals do when they come across a word they don't know?

1. **Use context clues.** Use the other words in the sentence to determine the meaning of the word.

2. **Take the word apart.** Does the word contain any prefixes, roots, or suffixes that you can use to help you figure out what it means?

3. **Look it up.** If you can't figure out what the word is on your own, Google it!

It Figures! (How to Figure Out Figurative Language.)

The English language is not always literal. Refresh your memory about the different types of figurative speech and see the most common figures of speech. See "Figures of Speech" at: www.StudySkills.com/bonus-edu

How to Learn Academic and "Domain-Specific" Words

In school, we call these "vocabulary words." If you haven't seen it already, see "How to Learn Vocabulary Words" at: www.StudySkills.com/bonus-edu.

Ask questions
-Summary-

1 **Knowing how to effectively communicate will make you successful in school and the workplace.** All communication relies on you knowing the purpose for your communication. Asking questions will help you determine your purpose for speaking, writing, listening, and comprehension.

2 **Having your teacher's support can benefit you and your grades in many ways.** Most teachers see 100 to 150 students every day. It is up to you to stand out from the crowd – in a positive way – by asking questions and participating in class.

3 **You can improve your reading speed and comprehension by "priming your brain" before you read.** To encourage the information you read to "stick," ask yourself a variety of questions before you begin reading.

4 **Questions also prime your brain for taking and studying notes.** The more prepared you are for class, the more you will be able to focus, identify important information to write down, and increase your retention. Questions also help you create a study guide out of your notes.

5 **The best way to prepare for tests is to consistently ask questions throughout a chapter or unit of study.** Creating questions out of the information helps your brain make the connections that are so important for recall.

6 **Questions can help you write papers, too.** Use questions to help you identify key information that your paper should address. These questions can then be transformed into starter sentences for paragraphs and help you organize your information.

7 **For oral presentations, turn your topics into questions.** Carefully prepare content in writings using keywords and phrases only. Practicing your presentation several times will allow you to be comfortable with your content and sound the most natural.

8 **When you have a language question, you need to know the right place to go to get answers.** Using our resources will help you get your questions answered.

Record your progress

Record your progress

Check all statements below that apply to you:

_____ I am sometimes shocked, and occasionally disappointed, by the grades I see on my report card.

_____ I always have good intentions of doing better in school, but I sometimes lose track of my goals.

_____ I have learned a lot of good information in this program; I'm just not sure where to start.

You will find solutions to these problems, and much more, in the following section.

> Spend more time examining yourself, and less time seeking the approval of others.

My life was transformed when I learned how to manage school and learning. The greatest – and most valuable – change came from the confidence I developed, the confidence that I can do anything I *want* to do!

I wrote this book because I want you to discover that same confidence! I want you to honor the natural skills, talents, and desires that make you unique. When you know how to set your own goals, organize, and learn effectively, nothing can stop you!

So far, all of the SOAR® strategies have been presented without interference from the real world. But life will throw you curve balls. You can have the best of intentions, but when the unexpected happens, it can throw you off course.

That's why this section is here. "Record your progress" is about having a plan in place to stay on track, or get back on track when needed. Here, you will pull together all the strategies you have learned…and blend them into your life.

Feelings Follow Action

You will feel discouraged from time to time. That's normal. Be kind to yourself. Trying to control feelings is like trying to stop the wind: it's impossible!

Focus, instead, on what you can control: your *actions*! In his book, *Constructive Living,* Dr. David K. Reynolds makes the point that no one really knows where feelings come from. We can identify things that *trigger* feelings. We can choose how we react to feelings. But, we can't control the actual feelings.

Instead, we challenge negative feelings through our actions. So if you feel discouraged, that's normal. Now do something about it! Before you know it, one or two small steps of positive action will transform your feelings*.

Taking action is the only way to develop a positive feeling about yourself and a positive attitude towards life. As Dr. Reynolds says, "Nobody can talk you into feeling good about yourself. You can get that solid good feeling from taking action…and being successful."

*For some people, positive action may not be enough. Be aware that this could be a sign of clinical depression or other illness requiring medical attention. Depression is a real condition: it is caused by an imbalance of chemicals in your brain. If "positive actions" only leave you feeling more and more discouraged, *take another action* and talk to a trusted adult about getting medical attention.

chapter 16

Tracking Your Grades

"Why Should I Keep Track of My Grades?"

If you have ever been surprised by a grade on your report card, you already know one reason why you should keep track of your own grades. Students often blame their teachers for "bad grades," but teachers don't *invent* grades –students earn them. While teachers offer assistance and may offer a point or two to boost your grade, 99.9% of the work rests on your shoulders. Tracking your own grades helps you see exactly how you earn your grade, what scores give your grade a boost, and what scores send you falling.

Tracking your own grades improves your grades! That's right, the process of tracking your scores allows you to see exactly how each point affects your grade. This knowledge will help you stay motivated about turning homework in on time, being a little more careful when answering test questions, etc. Unfortunately, low scores on one or two assignments can lower your grade *fast*. While it's not impossible to pull your grade back up, it can be difficult. It is far better to be proactive and prevent the slippery slope from starting.

Kutlayev Dmitry/Shutterstock

When you keep track of your own grades, you can catch any mistakes your teacher may have made. (It happens more often than you might think.) Have you ever seen the tiny boxes in which teachers have to record grades for each student? It is very easy to type the wrong grade in a slot, or perhaps simply type the number incorrectly. You can help your teacher stay accurate by recording your own grades, too.

One note of caution… If you think your teacher has made an error, be *very* polite about it! Say something like, "Mrs. Smith, I think there may be a problem with my grade," rather than, "Mrs. Smith, YOU made a mistake!" Do you see the difference?

Calculating your grades can sometimes save you work. You can often calculate the score you need on an upcoming test in order to receive a specific final grade. You can use this information to determine how much time you should spend studying.

For example, I once figured out that it did not matter if I earned an "A" or a "F" on my French final exam because I would still get a "B" for my final grade. So I used my time to study for other subjects. (As it turns out, I did so poorly on the final exam that my teacher actually called me at home to reassure me that I would still get a "B" on my report card. She was afraid I would be very upset. It was such a nice gesture; I didn't have the heart to tell her that it was part of my calculated plan.)

To summarize, tracking your own grades will allow you to:

- ☑ Avoid surprises on your report card.
- ☑ See how each assignment and every point can affect your grade.
- ☑ Gain a sense of control over your grades.
- ☑ Keep track of your teacher's records…teachers can make mistakes, too!
- ☑ Set more accurate goals for each test and assignment.

"How Do I Keep Track of My Grades?"

Most school systems allow students to see their grades online. If you have that service available, use it and check it regularly! Watch how your scores on assignments and tests affect your grade, check to make sure the scores you see online match the scores you earned, and use the information to set some goals for upcoming tests and projects. (Check your grades as part of your "Sunday Night Meeting.")

If your school does not offer this service, you can use the simple tracking sheet at www.StudySkills.com/bonus-edu to keep track of your grades. (See directions on the next page.) It takes time, but recording and calculating your grades is a good thing to do during those first few minutes of class, while waiting for the bell to ring and class to get started.

Calculating Your Grades

Directions: Use the table below to see how to keep track of your grades throughout a marking period. Refer to the steps that follow for a specific explanation.

Date	Assignment	# of points # of points possible	Total # of points Total points poss.	Percentage
9-10	Homework #1	$\frac{9}{10}$	$\frac{9}{10}$	90%
9-16	Homework #2	$\frac{8}{10}$	$\frac{9}{10} + \frac{8}{10} = \frac{17}{20}$	85%
9-30	Quiz #1	$\frac{20}{30}$	$\frac{17}{20} + \frac{20}{30} = \frac{37}{50}$	74%
10-8	Test #1	$\frac{50}{50}$	$\frac{37}{50} + \frac{50}{50} = \frac{87}{100}$	87%

Step 1:

Record each of your graded assignments as it is returned to you.

Step 2:

In the third column, write a fraction for the number of points you scored out of points possible for that assignment. In the shaded column, keep a running record of your grade by adding the new assignment points to the total points earned in the class up to that point. For example, this student scored 9 out of 10 points on Homework #1 and 8 out of 10 points on Homework #2. His total points possible after his 2nd homework assignment are 17 out of 20.

Step 3:

Use a calculator to calculate your current percentage score. You can figure this out by dividing your total points earned by total points possible. You will get a decimal. Multiply this decimal by 100 for your percent score (points earned / points possible x 100 = __ %).

Helpful Hint

For a downloadable Grade Tracking Sheet, go to www.StudySkills.com/bonus-edu. Print one for each class. Keep one copy in the front of each folder in your binder. As you get papers back, record the grades on your Tracking Sheet and place the corrected assignments behind it.

chapter 17
Monitoring Your Goals

There are many different type of goals: long-term career goals, things you would like to do sometime in your lifetime, things you would like to accomplish within a year, things you hope to do tomorrow, etc. All of these goals are an important part of inspiring you to achieve good grades.

When you have something to look forward to, it is much easier to stay motivated. For the purposes of this program, we will focus on two types of goals: your long-term goals for each marking period and your short-term goals for each week.

Beginning of Each Marking Period

Earlier in this book, you spent some time analyzing your goals. It is important to do this at the beginning of each semester when you have a clean slate and can have a fresh start!

Make a copy of the downloadable goal sheet from www.StudySkills.com/bonus-edu and post it somewhere where you will see it often: on the wall or a bulletin board in your room, the front pocket of your binder, even on the wall in your bathroom where you will see it every morning. The important thing is to put it in a place where you will see it often and consistently be reminded of what you want to achieve.

amasterphotographer/Shutterstock

Goals I Will Accomplish...

In order to achieve a healthy balance in your life, create a long-term goal for school, for your health, and for something outside of school. Reevaluate these goals at the beginning of each quarter/semester.

Remember the key to achieving your goals is to *take action*!

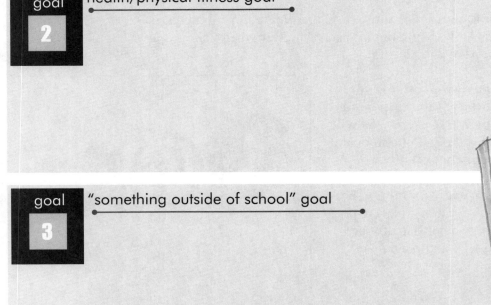

goal 1 ——— school goal

goal 2 ——— health/physical fitness goal

goal 3 ——— "something outside of school" goal

Post this page somewhere you will see it every day.
Use these long-term goals to help you determine your weekly goals.

Beginning of Each Week

The path toward reaching your long-term goals is paved with small actions. The best way to take these steps is to start each week with a bit of planning. At the beginning of the week (just before you talk to your parents about each of your schedules), review your planner to see what you have coming up the following week:

- ❑ **Record test and project dates in your planner** for the week (if you have not already done so).

- ❑ **Set three goals** for yourself for the week. (See *Weekly* Goals on the sample planner sheet on the next page.)

- ❑ **Schedule action steps.** Determine when you will complete these action steps and map them out in your planner.

Now that you have come to the last section of this book and learned many other strategies, it is appropriate to take another look at the sample planner page we saw in Section Two. Do you see how weekly planning automatically develops the routine of monitoring your goals?

A few minutes at the beginning of each week is all you need to revisit your goals and continue to plan how you will achieve them.

Flexibility Is Key

Your week will not turn out exactly as you plan. Sometimes you may have 1 or 2 days that fall off course, and other times it may be the whole week. When this happens, don't give up on your goals! Rely on your ability to make decisions according to your priorities, then get back on track as soon as possible. It may occasionally be a few weeks before you resume the habit of weekly planning...that's normal. Just don't give up on it permanently.

Conclusion

Setting, tracking, and achieving goals is *not* a one-time process. It is an on-going, cyclical process. For that reason, much of this chapter repeats information from Section Two. That's intentional.

Your goals will naturally grow and change over time. So it is important to develop the habit of reevaluating and planning for them on a regular basis.

Sept	3 Monday	4 Tuesday	5 Wednesday	6 Thursday	7 Friday	8 Saturday / 9 Sunday / Weekly Goals
1st hour	Page 161 #2-20 all					- Get homework done this morning (2 hours?)
2nd hour	None					
3rd hour	Get Permission Slip Signed					
4th hour	None					
5th hour						**9 Sunday**
6th hour	Study for Chapter 4 Test on Thurs.			Science test today		Grandma's b-day lunch 1 p.m.
7th hour	Read section 5.2. Questions pg. 109					
Other	Math book Science book Language Arts book					**Weekly Goals**
3 p.m.	Snack	Movie Club Mtg. Snack	Snack	Snack	Snack	
4 p.m.	Shoot hoops & run	Shoot hoops & run	Review all notes for 15 minutes/ Do Math	Shoot hoops & run	Review all notes for 15 minutes	- Shoot hoops and run three days this week
5 p.m.	Review all notes for 15 minutes/ Do Math	Review all notes for 15 minutes/ Do Math	Study 15 min. for Science test	Review all notes for 15 minutes/ Do Math	No other homework tonight!	- Review notes every day
6 p.m.	Study Science 15 min. L. Arts HW (1 hr)	Study 20 min. for Science test				
7 p.m.					Football game	- Have at least two hours of homework-free time every evening!
8 p.m.	Watch TV Show at 8:30					
9 -10 p.m.	10:30 Read in bed/Sleep	10:30 Read in bed/Sleep	10:30 Read in bed/Sleep	10:30 Read in bed/ Sleep		

chapter 18
Recognizing Your Achievements

There is nothing like the satisfaction of accomplishing something you worked hard to achieve! However, as human beings, we naturally notice and focus on negative things much more than positive, which means it is easy to get discouraged when you encounter setbacks. You must make it a point to counteract your negative thoughts and acknowledge every little achievement along the way towards achieving your goals.

At the end of each day, take a moment to think about the positive things you accomplished. If you had a bad day and can't think of a single token of success, ask yourself, "What did I *learn* from my experiences today?" This reflection is a great way to maintain a positive attitude, even during very difficult times.

At the end of each week, take a moment to look back on the week and make note of the progress you made, even if it was a small fraction of what you planned. Taking this time will help you to stay motivated. You'll also develop the skills and attitudes that will help you be successful throughout your life.

It is impossible to take on all of the strategies in this book at the same time; you have to take baby steps with a few ideas that fit you and your needs best. After you have experienced success with one or two techniques, you will naturally try more. I encourage you to revisit this book often and enjoy the process of making schoolwork – and life – easier for you.

Conclusion

There used to be a public service commercial targeted to smokers who were struggling to kick the habit. It encouraged them by saying, "Don't quit quitting!" In the world of SOAR® Study Skills, the message for you is, "Don't quit **S**etting goals. Don't quit **O**rganizing. Don't quit **A**sking questions…." You get the idea!

In the meantime, take a few moments to think back to the information you have learned from this program and select the top three things you would like to try within the next month. **R**ecord them on the next page and begin immediately! Good luck!

After you hit the home run...

...you still have to run the bases.

In baseball, you can hit the ball out of the park, but the run is not added to your score until you run to 1st, 2nd, 3rd base...and then back to home plate.

Congratulations! You've hit a "home run" by completing this book. But the strategies in this book won't do anything for you...unless you use them. You still have to run the bases! In the spaces below, describe three strategies from this book that you will do (or continue to do) to help you get better grades in less time.

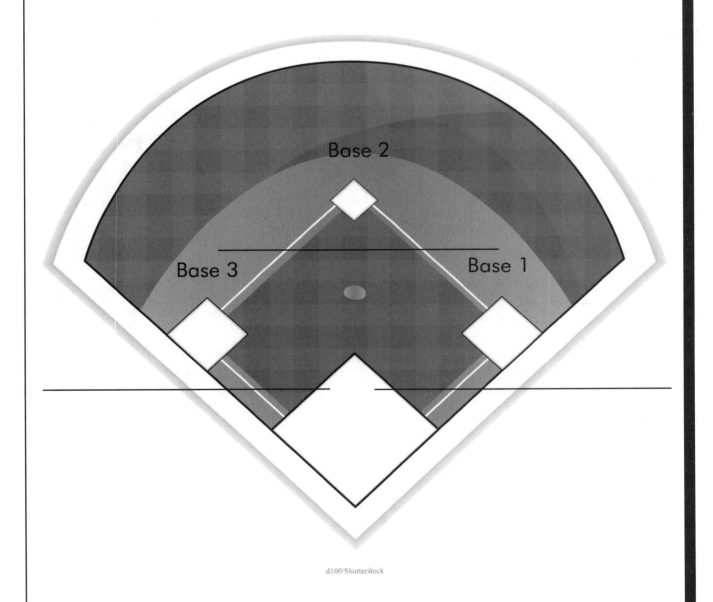

Base 2

Base 3

Base 1

d100/Shutterstock

Directions: This photo is for use with the activity in Chapter 10.

Look at it for no more than 5 seconds!

Now turn to page 160!

<u>Directions</u>: These questions are for use with the activity in Chapter 10.

① What is centered directly above the man's head?

② What toy is directly above his left shoulder (on the right side of the photo)?

③ Was the snake hanging over his head striped or spotted?

④ How many times is the word "light" visible in this photo?

⑤ How many fish are in the package on the right side of the picture?

Answers:
① slingshot
② *Pirate Collection*
③ spotted
④ three
⑤ four